Our Healing
God-With-Us

*Gospel Images
for Prayer*

MATTHEW

by Robert L. Knopp

Foreword by Robert F. Morneau

Pauline
BOOKS & MEDIA

Nihil Obstat:
Rev. Thomas W. Buckley, STD, SSL

Imprimatur:
†Bernard Cardinal Law
Archbishop of Boston
June 10, 1996

Cover design: Sergia Ballini, FSP

ISBN 0-8198-3086-0

Printed and published in the U.S.A. by Pauline Books & Media, 50 Saint Pauls Avenue, Boston MA 02130-3491.

http://www.pauline.org

Pauline Books & Media is the publishing house of the Daughters of St. Paul, an international congregation of women religious serving the Church with the communications media.

Contents

Foreword

A fierce battle is taking place in our culture regarding the imagination. Nor is this a *cold* war but one of extreme passion and intensity. The importance of victory cannot be exaggerated because the images we create or absorb shape our inner attitudes, which in turn radically influence our lifestyle and behavior. It's a simple syllogism but one which has profound ramifications.

Images come from multiple sources: television, songs, movies, magazines, science, poetry, lived lives. Within the Christian community a major source stimulating the imagination is sacred Scripture. God's word often draws pictures for us that contain values and virtues that lead us to the kingdom: Jesus as good shepherd; our spirituality as one of mutual self-giving as depicted in the vine and the branches; the separation of the sheep and the goats based on our treatment of one another; God as the potter shaping and molding our lives.

In a world filled with incredible violence, the Christian community continues to offer an alternative to the culture of death. Ours is to be a culture of love, a "civilization of love," in which every single human being is invited to the wedding feast and must be treated with awesome respect. The poet Gerard Manley Hopkins calls us "immortal diamonds." Our images must offer realistic hope.

It is not enough to encounter an image, symbol, metaphor or story. More is required. We must assimilate and appropriate these formative sights and sounds until they are absorbed into our spiritual bloodstream. This will require prayer and reflection as well as commitment to translate them into action. Our process of formation and conversion takes time and much grace. Perseverance in prayer is essential to Christian maturity.

This volume, like its three companions, is about discipleship and how we respond to that call by using biblical images. Robert Knopp looks deeply into each of the Gospels and extracts for us images that give us access to the person of Jesus. Each Gospel is unique in its approach to the Lord but all are the same in inviting us to know, love and serve him with all of our being.

In *Our Healing God-With-Us*, we come to see Jesus as our God who is with us, "Emmanuel." Through the parables and narrative accounts, Jesus comes to us as Savior, the new Moses, the wise teacher, the great healer, the builder of a new Church, our final judge. By pondering these images and mysteries through prayer, hopefully we will conform our lives to Christ Jesus, our saving-God-with-us.

One last word about images, the cornerstone of this book. Avery Dulles, in his influential book *Models of the Church*, writes: "Symbols transform the horizons of man's life, integrate his perception of reality, alter his scale of values, reorient his loyalties, attachments, and aspirations in a manner far exceeding the powers of abstract conceptual thought." No more need be said about the power of images and their possible transformative influence on our lives.

†Robert F. Morneau
Auxiliary Bishop of Green Bay

Invitation

Together let's look into Matthew's Gospel to ponder and pray, as Vatican II urged us:

Learn by frequent reading of the divine Scriptures the "excellent knowledge of Jesus Christ" (Phil 3:8).... Prayer should accompany the reading of sacred Scripture, so that God and man may talk together; for "we speak to him when we pray; we hear him when we read the divine saying" (*Dogmatic Constitution on Divine Revelation*, no. 25, quoting St. Ambrose).

This small book, like its predecessor, *Mark: A Very Human Jesus*, concentrates on the images—expressed or implied—in which the Gospel presents Jesus and his message. For, more than abstractions, images stir our hearts to pray.

Imagery usually appeals to our senses through rich color, form and sound, but the evangelists offer us no descriptive details of Jesus' external appearance and few such images of his actions. They prefer the symbolic imagery of narratives and parables that suggest the spiritual sense or inner mystery of Jesus' life, words and actions. Through such images Matthew invites us to enter prayerfully into this mystery. I have therefore divided his Gospel into units in which I find a central image or cluster of images that stir our musing. I express my own musings in free-flowing, often rhythmic sense lines, hopefully harmonizing with Matthew's tone in response to his implied invitation to pray.

According to the leading source theory of biblical scholars, Mark wrote first; then Matthew and Luke repeated, summarized, expanded or revised nearly all his content as a primary source for their Gospels. Since I have already explored Mark's images, I have resisted repeating them here, except where necessary to maintain context and coherence, or where Matthew introduces substantial changes. This decision allows us to focus upon what is either original in Matthew's Gospel or culled from another source that many scholars believe Luke also used, a lost source they call "Q."

Matthew presents Jesus in a wide range of images and roles:

the Savior of his people promised by the prophets (Mt 1:21-23) and Savior of the Gentiles as well (2:1-12);

the new Moses returning from Egypt to save his people (2:19-21);

mediator of the new law of love on the mountain (ch. 5);

the wise teacher of the way to God our Father (chs. 6-7);

the great healer who cures "every disease and illness" (9:35);

the sensitive counselor, "gentle and humble in heart" (11:29);

the Son of Man who has "nowhere to lay his head" (8:20);

the Son of God who alone "knows the Father" (11:27) and whom only the Father can reveal to Peter as Messiah (16:17);

the builder of a new Church as entry into "the kingdom of heaven" (16:18-19; 28:16-20);

our final judge who severely warns us against sin (25:30, 46),

yet lovingly identifies himself with the poor (25:35-40);

our saving God-with-us (1:23) "until the end of the age" (28:20).

This comprehensive vision of Jesus makes it difficult to characterize Matthew's Gospel. He is perhaps best distinguished from the other evangelists by the supreme reverence with which he constantly depicts Jesus, apparently in conscious or subconscious association with his unique identification of Jesus as Isaiah's "Emmanuel," which means "God is with us" (cf. 1:23).

Matthew's many summaries of Mark's passages focus so intently upon key revelations about

Jesus that they give the impression Matthew stands farther off from Jesus, in reverent awe. Matthew confirms and enhances this impression in many of the Gospel's original narratives by the way he depicts Jesus: even as an infant, Jesus is worshiped by the wise men; in his opening Sermon on the Mount, he teaches with awe-inspiring authority; walking like Yahweh upon the sea, he saves Peter from drowning; he majestically confers upon Peter the power of the keys to the kingdom of heaven; he tells a parable of the mighty Lord of the vineyard who generously rewards workers as he freely wills; he foretells his coming in glory to judge the nations; finally, he shares his saving power with his apostles and assures them he will be with them "to the end of the age."

As these passages suggest, Matthew constantly leads us into prayer. In his opening chapters he can move us to speak to God as did Joseph struggling to make the right decision, or Mary bearing the infant Jesus in her arms. By telling us the child is to be named Jesus because "he will save his people from their sins" (1:21), Matthew suggests we thank the Father for sending his Son to save us, declare our faith in Mary's son as our saving Lord, and ask the Spirit to bring forth Jesus in us. By calling Jesus "Emmanuel," Matthew suggests we pray to him, not primarily as the infant in Mary's arms or the risen Lord of glory with his Father in heaven, but as the saving Lord who lives with us. Mark hardly dealt with the question of Jesus' continued presence with his followers after his ascension, but Matthew evidently considers this question pivotal. In his very first narrative he combines the names "Jesus" and "Emmanuel" to open a dominant chord of his Gospel: *Jesus is our saving God-with-us.*

He reinforces this chord in many texts: "Whoever welcomes you *welcomes me*" (10:40); "*Come to me...*and I will give you rest" (11:28); "Where two or three are gathered in my name, *I am there among them*" (18:20); "As you did it to one of the least of these...*you did it to me*" (25:40). Matthew's fascination with the presence of Jesus in our lives as a truly human being yet at the same time our saving God-with-us runs beneath the surface of his Gospel, setting its tone and assuring its unity.

In my own reading of Matthew I find his vision of Jesus our saving God-with-us becoming a dominant image in my prayer. Of course, it need not be the same for you. My prayer may sometimes speak for you, but prayer is so personal that yours must flow from your own heart in your own words—or no words at all.

In the relatively few passages over which Christian churches still differ, I have adhered to the Catholic Church's interpretation of the apostolic traditions that gave rise to the New Testament. Though the Church has rarely interpreted individual verses, it provides an overall understanding of Scripture through the kerygma and its corollary doctrines, roughed out by the apostles themselves (as suggested in Acts 15 and some later passages of the New Testament, such as 2 Pt 1:16-21 and 3:16), and refined by the early Fathers of the Church and the councils.

I lovingly dedicate this book to my wife Marian, always the dearest partisan of my efforts.

Now enter with me into Matthew's Gospel to ponder over one image or set of images each day, letting it grow into prayer. As we begin, let's ask St. Matthew to pray for us and invoke the Holy Spirit, to inspire us to find Matthew's healing God-with-us.

The
Infancy Narrative

Jesus' Family Tree

Mt 1:1-17: *An account of the genealogy of Jesus the Messiah, the son of David, the son of Abraham.*

Abraham was the father of Isaac, and Isaac the father of Jacob, and Jacob the father of Judah...and Judah the father of Perez...by Tamar...and Salmon the father of Boaz by Rahab, and Boaz the father of Obed by Ruth....

And David was the father of Solomon by the wife of Uriah....

And after the deportation to Babylon: Jechoniah was the father of Salathiel...and Jacob the father of Joseph the husband of Mary, of whom Jesus was born...the Messiah.

So all the generations from Abraham to David are fourteen generations; and from David to the deportation to Babylon, fourteen generations; and from the deportation to Babylon to the Messiah, fourteen generations.

To contemplate:

Thanks, Matthew, for your effort
   to trace Jesus' family tree
all the way back to Abraham,
   father of all the chosen—

chosen himself by Yahweh to begin
　　this line of high and low,
　　of men and women,
　　saints and sinners.
Thus you firmly fix the Messiah,
　　as Savior of our race,
within the generations of our kind,
　　rooted in great and small.
Your Jesus is a man among us all—
　　a Jew among Jews,
　　great among the great,
　　small among the small.
You number him among the members,
　　biblical seven as your base,
the number that means "complete,"
　　number among all numbers
　　with meaning above the rest.
Yet your Jesus is not just a seven;
　　he's a fourteen, a double seven—
　　even a triple double seven—
the triple-double-seventh child
　　of the father of the chosen,
　　father of saints and sinners.

Jesus, I revere you, man among us all,
　　God's promised of our kind!

Joseph's Dream

Mt 1:18-21: *When his mother Mary had been engaged to Joseph, but before they lived together, she was found to be with child from the Holy Spirit. Her husband Joseph, being a righteous man and unwilling to expose her to public disgrace, planned to dismiss her quietly. But just when he had resolved to do this, an angel of the Lord appeared to him in a dream and said, "Joseph, son of David, do not be afraid to take Mary as your wife, for the child conceived in her is from the Holy Spirit. She will bear a son, and you are to name him Jesus, for he will save his people from their sins."*

To contemplate:

How did Joseph, that holy man,
    feel at the sight of Mary pregnant,
knowing in his secret heart
    she carried not his child?
Mary, his own dear wife-to-be,
    of all women his cherished one,
who'd always been so true to him,
    so modest, pure, and so reserved—

how could she now betray the trust
    he had so tenderly placed in her?
Yet there it was for all to see,
    her bosom swelling day by day.

Should he denounce her publicly
    and thereby put her at fatal risk
of stern Mosaic law of stoning?
    No, he'd not disgrace her publicly;
he'd simply break the promise-bond.
    But just as God did not forsake
his first Joseph, Egypt's slave,
    the Lord now sends angelic herald
to comfort this second saintly dreamer
    with amazing truth of Mary's son:
not by man has she conceived,
    but by the power of the Holy Spirit
she now bears the one who will save
    his people from their sins!

Then faithful Joseph must have said:
    "O Mary, mother of holy child,
God's chosen one to bear his Son—
    gift to us all of his Holy Spirit,
to save us from our sins—O Mary,
    come and live with me—my wife!"

Emmanuel

Mt 1:22-23: *All this took place to fulfill what had been spoken by the Lord through the prophet:*
    "Look, the virgin shall conceive and bear a son,
        and they shall name him Emmanuel,"
which means, "God is with us."

To contemplate:

The Lord himself spoke long ago,
   through the great Isaiah
to tell his plan to save our race
   and be our God-with-us.
The helpless child in Mary's womb
   confirms that God is with her,
just as any mother's child
   assures her of God's love.
But this child is more than surety;
   this child is very God!
The same God for whom Isaiah spoke,
   the God who would be with us—
this God alive in Mary's womb,
   her child sharing her flesh,

daily growing in length and breadth—
   great God, her tiny babe!

O Jesus, babe in Mary's womb,
   God's Christmas gift to us,
we humbly wait your coming forth
   to dwell at last with us.
Yet there in Mary's loving heart,
   blest daughter of our race,
Joseph's true and faithful spouse—
   you already dwell with us.
And just as in her heart you dwell,
   in my poor heart you live,
source of my inner life of grace,
   God's Christmas gift to me.
The giver of all good gifts to us
   becomes the gift himself.
Jesus, son of sweetest Mary,
   is truly God-with-us.
O Jesus, save us all from sin
   and be our God-with-us—
   my saving God-with-me!

God Is with Us

Mt 1:21-23: *"She will bear a son, and you are to name him Jesus, for he will save his people from their sins." All this took place to fulfill what had been spoken by the Lord through the prophet:*
"Look, the virgin shall conceive and bear a son,
and they shall name him Emmanuel,"
which means, "God is with us."

To contemplate:

O Matthew, you inspire my prayer
    to Jesus as man-with-me,
true member of our human race
    from Abraham descended.
Yet, much more than man is he—
    you call him Emmanuel,
foretold so many years ago
    by Israel's great prophet.
How would you have me pray to him?
    As to my very brother?
Or as the God far off from me,
    Creator of my life?
As both, you surely say to me.

As brother who shares with me
my joys, my sorrows, trials, and death—
    yet saves me from my sins.
Saves me because he's also God.
    Yet because he's brother, too;
he's not a God who's far away,
    but even God-with-me.
So I picture him before me here,
    as human as I,
yet also the God who created me,
    man-and-God-with-me!

Jesus, within my very heart,
    the God who in me dwells,
loving me as your own child,
    yet loving me as brother.
In reaching you who are the man,
    I touch my God himself!
You have a name that signifies
    you are both God and man;
it is "Jesus, our Emmanuel"—
    our man-and-God-with-us!

The Virgin Mary Bore a Son

Mt 1:24-25: *When Joseph awoke from sleep, he did as the angel of the Lord commanded him; he took her as his wife, but had no marital relations with her until she had borne a son; and he named him Jesus.*

To contemplate:

"He took her as his wife."
How terse your sentence, Matthew,
    He took her as his wife,
and she who was a virgin bride,
    became the virgin mother
of the saving "God-is-with-us."
    Jesus, we pause in awe
at your birth, marvelous birth
    from marvelous conception
through the Holy Spirit—Spirit-God!

"She bore a son"—so brief a note
    to tell the greatest birth
of all the ages of our race—
    your birth, my saving Lord!

Matthew, you've outdone yourself
    in brevity. No detail,
not a single image to help us see
    the birth of our Emmanuel!

Yet you have said enough to keep
    us marveling for all ages,
marveling at the only birth
    of son of virgin mother.
You leave our imagination free
    to make our own details.

We watch the adoring holy man,
    embrace God's own command
to take as wife the pregnant maid,
    adoring now her little child,
embracing him, though not his own.

We watch the adoring holy maid,
    hold close her holy child
conceived through the Holy Spirit—
    the promised Son of God!
    And we adore him, too....

Jesus' Holy Family

Mt 1:24-25: *Joseph...did as the angel of the Lord commanded him; he took her as his wife, but had no marital relations with her until she had borne a son; and he named him Jesus.*

To contemplate:

Joseph took her as his wife,
yet sacrificed his husband's right
    until she gave birth to the son
he named the "Savior of our race."
    And then did Joseph love his wife
and give her other children dear?
    Our word "until" suggests just that,
though Matthew's Greek does not.
    Sweet as marital act would be,
and dear to engender his own heirs,
    yet dearer far this holy child
without a peer in all the world!
    Their marriage was beyond the way
of covenant of man and wife—
    a union like no other bond,
rich indwelling of the Spirit-God.

So rich, it was a holy sign
of heaven's spiritual kingdom
   living in their humble home
in the person of God's Son.

This was the faith of early Church,
of learned Fathers and humble folk:
   Mary remained the virgin mother,
Joseph the guardian of his Lord.
   For this belief Jesus himself
prepared the ground by giving praise
   to sacrifice of marriage act
"for the sake of heaven's kingdom" (Mt 19:12).
   And so the Church presents to us
a vision of Jesus' family
   as Mary's ever virgin love
and Joseph's loving abstinence,
   in mutual spiritual sign
of love greater than their own—
   the love of God the Father
for his only Son, for Mary's only son.
Father, fill us with your love for him!

Follow the Star!

Mt 2:1-9: *In the time of King Herod, after Jesus was born in Bethlehem of Judea, wise men from the East came to Jerusalem, asking, "Where is the child who has been born king of the Jews? For we observed his star at its rising, and have come to pay him homage." When King Herod heard this, he was frightened, and all Jerusalem with him; and calling together all the chief priests and scribes of the people, he inquired of them where the Messiah was to be born. They told him, "In Bethlehem of Judea; for so it has been written by the prophet...." Then Herod secretly called for the wise men and...sent them to Bethlehem, saying, "Go and search diligently for the child; and when you have found him, bring word so that I may also go and pay him homage." When they had heard the king, they set out; and there, ahead of them, went the star.*

To contemplate:

The king is he who should be wise,
   wiser than the ones he rules.
Yet these Gentiles—Eastern men
   see the star the king sees not,
      follow dreams of greater thing
   than great King Herod dares to dream—
the thing he fears above all else:
the rising of a greater king,
   a king foretold by ancient prophets,
      a king who would displace the kings
of earth with another kind of kingdom,
far greater than earth's puny states (Dan 2:44).

Yet Herod hides his fears from them
   and asks his wisest priests and scribes
      the birthplace of Messiah-King;
   they relate great Micah's prophecy
of Bethlehem, town of David's line.
With false intent, the frightened king
   sends them forth to follow a star,
      their star of dreams of greater things
   than a wicked king can ever dream,
as he frets at home within his fort.
Jesus, you are the brightest star
   of all our dreams; I'll follow you—
      follow you wherever you lead,
   follow where you alone can lead.
Help me follow, forever follow you!

Wise Men Find Jesus with Mary

Mt 2:9-12: *When they had heard the king, they set out; and there, ahead of them, went the star that they had seen at its rising, until it stopped over the place where the child was. When they saw that the star had stopped, they were overwhelmed with joy. On entering the house, they saw the child with Mary his mother; and they knelt down and paid him homage. Then, opening their treasure chests, they offered him gifts of gold, frankincense, and myrrh. And having been warned in a dream not to return to Herod, they left for their own country by another road.*

To contemplate:

Those who are wise follow their dreams,
dreams like stars that light the night
and lead the way to a greater life,
a life with the one who *made* the light.
To follow the star is a joyful quest;
these wise are "overwhelmed with joy,"
the joy of the journey to find the child
who will change the world, change our lives.
And where do they find the maker of stars?

Where else but with his mother Mary,
the virgin who gave him virgin birth,
　　the mother God made by God for his own Son!

Down they kneel before little child
　　lying in mother Mary's arms.
They open the chests they've borne so long
　　to offer him earth's finest treasures.
First gold, the metal that gleams and fires
　　desires of people down the years—
they offer him gold that gives glint to kings,
　　the sign that he is the King of kings!
Then frankincense, the precious gum
　　that burns honor to the gods of men—
they offer him the aromatic scent
　　as sign they adore him as their God.
And finally myrrh, bitter-tasting balm,
　　used to embalm and bury the dead—
they offer him myrrh that signifies
　　he's vulnerable to death, like us.

O Jesus, child of mother Mary,
　　with her and Joseph and these wise men—
Jesus, wiser than the wise who seek you—
　　I offer you not gold or incense,
　　only the myrrh of humanity.

Jesus Is the New Israel

Mt 2:13-15: *Now after they had left, an angel of the Lord appeared to Joseph in a dream and said, "Get up, take the child and his mother, and flee to Egypt, and remain there until I tell you; for Herod is about to search for the child, to destroy him." Then Joseph got up, took the child and his mother by night, and went to Egypt, and remained there until the death of Herod. This was to fulfill what had been spoken by the Lord through the prophet, "Out of Egypt I have called my son."*

To contemplate:

Why, Matthew, tell us a story
   of Jesus fleeing to Egypt?
What meaning can Egypt have
   for the Savior of the world?
Only that God may call him back:
   "Out of Egypt I called my son,"
quoting: "When Israel was a child...
   out of Egypt I called my son" (Hos 11:1).

Thus you say in your story-way
   Jesus relives the very life
of his own people, Israel,
   whom he will save from slavery.
So we picture him in Mary's arms,
   fleeing on Joseph's lowly burro
from the evil Herod, figure now
   of Evil pursuing Good to death.
And surely, Matthew, you think of him
   as embodiment of humankind,
of all the people he will save,
   pursued by Satan unto death.
This is the child of strangest promise:
   Israel's prophets from of old
foretold he'd suffer all his people
   had to suffer in slavery.
This is the child who will fulfill
   the dreams of all the Jews,
of all the peoples of the world—
   of all our dreams as well.

O Jesus, child in Mary's arms,
   led by faithful Joseph
into exile from your home—
   Jesus, child of dreams,
I believe you embody God's great love
   for all of us today.

Jesus Returns in a New Exodus

Mt 2:16-23: *When Herod saw that he had been tricked by the wise men, he was infuriated, and he sent and killed all the children in and around Bethlehem.... Then was fulfilled what had been spoken through the prophet Jeremiah:*

"A voice was heard in Ramah, wailing and loud lamentation,

Rachel weeping for her children; she refused to be consoled,

because they are no more."

When Herod died, an angel of the Lord suddenly appeared in a dream to Joseph in Egypt and said, "Get up, take the child and his mother, and go to the land of Israel, for those who were seeking the child's life are dead." Then Joseph got up, took the child and his mother, and went to the land of Israel.... After being warned in a dream, he went away to the district of Galilee. There he made his home in a town called Nazareth, so that what had been spoken through the prophets might be fulfilled, "He will be called a Nazorean."

To contemplate:

You offer us more images,
Matthew, stronger images:
of Herod in mad fury
killing little children,
and Jeremiah prophesying
of Rachel, Israel's mother,
crying for her children,
foreshadowing grief
of innocent people—
all the suffering
Jesus will bear
at whipping post,
on cruel cross,
for all our sins.
Then Joseph dreams again,
a dream of going home
to land of Israel,
land of promise—
God-sent dream
of going home,
true home with Jesus.
Thus, as our new Moses
he will lead us
on a new Exodus
out of exile,
to the new freedom
that all the prophets
down the ages dreamed.
O Jesus, our God-with-us, lead us home to you!

The
Public Ministry
of **Jesus**

The Messiah Will Divide the Chaff from the Wheat

Mt 3:1-12: *In those days John the Baptist appeared in the wilderness of Judea, proclaiming, "Repent, for the kingdom of heaven has come near...." ...John wore clothing of camel's hair with a leather belt around his waist, and his food was locusts and wild honey. Then the people of Jerusalem and all Judea were going out to him, and all the region along the Jordan, and they were baptized by him in the river Jordan, confessing their sins.*

But when he saw many Pharisees and Sadducees coming for baptism, he said to them, "You brood of vipers! Who warned you to flee from the wrath to come? Bear fruit worthy of repentance. Do not presume to say to yourselves, 'We have Abraham as our ancestor'; for I tell you, God is able from these stones to raise up children to Abraham. Even now the ax is lying at the root of the trees; every tree therefore that does not bear good fruit is cut down and thrown into the fire.

"I baptize you with water for repentance, but one who is more powerful than I is coming after me; I am not worthy to carry his sandals. He will baptize you with the Holy Spirit and fire. His winnowing fork is in his hand, and he will clear his threshing floor and will

gather his wheat into the granary; but the chaff he will burn with unquenchable fire."

To contemplate:

Fierce John appears upon the scene,
    proclaiming day of reckoning,
    day of separating bad trees
        from the good.
Like a new Elijah, John now warns
    the hypocrites who, like vipers,
    snake their way among the people,
        corrupting them.

John promises his water baptism
    will be followed by a greater
    with the Holy Spirit and fire,
        by one stronger than John,
the one who will toss the harvest crop
    into the strong dividing wind—
    the wind of the Holy Spirit—
        with dividing fork.

This mightier one than John
    will clear his threshing floor,
    make room for the good grain
        and let the bad chaff blow
        into the fiery void of hell!

    O Jesus, mighty harvester,
        renew us with your Spirit!

Jesus Humbly Embraces
His Father's Will

Mt 3:13-17: *Then Jesus came from Galilee to John at the Jordan, to be baptized by him. John would have prevented him, saying, "I need to be baptized by you, and do you come to me?" But Jesus answered him, "Let it be so now; for it is proper for us in this way to fulfill all righteousness." Then he consented. And when Jesus had been baptized, just as he came up from the water, suddenly the heavens were opened to him and he saw the Spirit of God descending like a dove and alighting on him. And a voice from heaven said, "This is my Son, the Beloved, with whom I am well pleased."*

To contemplate:

At last the Lord of all the world
    appears, a full-grown man.
He comes to join the sinners' line
    to be baptized by John.
John sees in him the mighty one
    and asks for his baptism.
But this great Lord of all the world
    submits himself to John.

Matthew's Jesus now speaks a word,
    his first word of wisdom:
"It is right for us to take the way
    the Father has set for us."
God's way is not the our human way of men,
    not even John the Baptist's way;
God's way is humble, unassuming—
    humbler than our human ways.

His Jesus descends into the water,
    that John might baptize him.
That this was God's way, God himself
    now ratifies in vision:
he opens the heavens and Jesus sees
    God's Spirit, like a dove,
alight upon him—Dove of peace,
    of deepest joy and love.
The Father himself declares of him:
    "This is my own dear Son;
with him I am divinely pleased—
    I love my own dear Son!"

O Jesus, baptized in Jordan stream,
    your baptism with the Spirit
gives me your same indwelling Dove Spirit,
    and God for my own Father!

Jesus Endures Temptations

Mt 4:1-11: *Then Jesus was led up by the Spirit into the wilderness to be tempted by the devil. He fasted forty days and forty nights, and afterwards he was famished. The tempter came and said to him, "If you are the Son of God, command these stones to become loaves of bread." But he answered, "It is written,*

'One does not live by bread alone,

but by every word that comes from the mouth of God.'"

Then the devil took him to the holy city and placed him on the pinnacle of the temple, saying to him, "If you are the Son of God, throw yourself down; for it is written,

'He will command his angels concerning you,'

and 'On their hands they will bear you up,

so that you will not dash your foot against a stone.'"

Jesus said to him, "Again it is written, 'Do not put the Lord your God to the test.'"

Again, the devil took him to a very high mountain and showed him all the kingdoms of the world and their splendor; and he said to him, "All these I will give you, if you will fall down and worship me." Jesus said to him, "Away with you, Satan! for it is written,

'Worship the Lord your God, and serve only him.'"

Then the devil left him, and suddenly angels came and waited on him.

To contemplate:

Led by the Spirit, Jesus walks
   into the desert, stark and grave,
      for holy fast and holy prayer,
         and tempting by the evil one:
"Why so hard upon yourself?
   Why deny good things of earth?
      If you are the Creator's Son,
         prove it—turn these stones to bread."
But Jesus lives more by an inner bread
   that sustains his every thought and act—
      the bread of God's own word for us.
"Why spend your life and energy
   teaching the dull the way of life?
      Win them by spectaculars,
         daring leap and angels' catch."
"No! Test not the Lord your God!"
"You want the whole world, do you not?
   The world is mine, mine to give,
      if bowing down, you worship me!"
      The most satanic test of all!
"'The Lord alone shall you adore,'"
   quotes Jesus from the word of God.
O Jesus, you *are* one of us—
   tempted even as we have been!

Jesus Is Light in the Darkness

Mt 4:12-17: *When Jesus heard that John had been arrested, he withdrew to Galilee. He left Nazareth and made his home in Capernaum by the sea, in the territory of Zebulun and Naphtali, so that what had been spoken through the prophet Isaiah might be fulfilled:*

"Land of Zebulun, land of Naphtali,

   on the road by the sea, across the Jordan, Galilee of the Gentiles—

   the people who sat in darkness have seen a great light,

   and for those who sat in the region and shadow of death light has dawned."

From that time Jesus began to proclaim, "Repent, for the kingdom of heaven has come near."

To contemplate:

Matthew's Jesus leaves his Nazareth home
   for a new home in Capernaum by the sea.
What must have been his parting word to Mary?
   And what her tearful parting word to him?

Into the land of Galilee he must go,
   the land where ten of Israel's tribes were lost

into the hands of their conquerors faithless eastern
     hordes.
   Long has he prepared for this great task,
the plan his Father wisely designed for him:
   long years of learning prayer at Mary's knee;
long years of childhood play and young man's work
   under Joseph's watchful eye and steady hand.
He submits to John's baptism in the Jordan
   and lastly conquers Satan's fierce temptations.

And now that John the Baptist's been arrested,
   now that the people have no guiding light,
he comes at last to cast the brightest light
   this land has ever seen or ever will.

His message simple, yet wisely to the point:
   "Repent, for heaven's kingdom is at hand,"
the kingdom Daniel said would smash all others,
   but never be itself destroyed (Dan 2:44).

You yourself, my Lord, are that great kingdom:
   Matthew said your name means "God is with us."
I long to follow, like the wise, the star,
   to repent of all dark thoughts and words and deeds,
to turn at last toward the light of all the world,
   and find you, the Light in whom God made all
      light!

Mt 4:18-22 = Mk 1:16-20 (the symbol "=" here signifies approxi-
mately parallel passages, presented in Mark: A Very Human
Jesus). *In this passage Jesus calls his first disciples.*

Jesus Teaches and Heals

Mt 4:23-25: *Jesus went throughout Galilee, teaching in their synagogues and proclaiming the good news of the kingdom and curing every disease and every sickness among the people. So his fame spread throughout all Syria, and they brought to him all the sick, those who were afflicted with various diseases and pains, demoniacs, epileptics, and paralytics, and he cured them. And great crowds followed him from Galilee, the Decapolis, Jerusalem, Judea, and from beyond the Jordan.*

To contemplate:

Now let it run through all the land—
   the good news of the kingdom—
      the news of cures of all disease,
        the news of Jesus' care.
No sickness is beyond his skill,
   no pain beyond his reach,
      and demons, too, he dominates
        with word of matchless might.

See him touch a festering wound,
stoop to lift a drooping head.
Watch him cure an epileptic,
animate a paralytic!
Between his cures he teaches them,
teaches how to live their lives,
to rise above the level field,
reaching for his high ideal.
Tireless he travels up the road
and down the hills and vales.
Tireless he travels Galilee
to make God's kingdom come.
Never have these people seen
a healer strong as he.
Never have these people heard
a teacher wise as he!

Jesus, God's kingdom come in person,
heal me of my many ills;
teach me the surest way, your way
to the kingdom you have brought.
Jesus, God's kingdom come in person,
cast out my evil demons;
teach me the wisdom of your way
and make me whole, like you.

Jesus Teaches True Happiness

Mt 5:1-10: *When Jesus saw the crowds, he went up the mountain; and after he sat down, his disciples came to him. Then he began to speak, and taught them, saying:*

"Blessed are the poor in spirit, for theirs is the kingdom of heaven.

"Blessed are those who mourn, for they will be comforted.

"Blessed are the meek, for they will inherit the earth.

"Blessed are those who hunger and thirst for righteousness, for they will be filled.

"Blessed are the merciful, for they will receive mercy.

"Blessed are the pure in heart, for they will see God.

"Blessed are the peacemakers, for they will be called children of God.

"Blessed are those who are persecuted for righteousness' sake, for theirs is the kingdom of heaven."

To contemplate:

A new Moses on a new mountain
   tells us God's holy will;
Wisdom himself tells all the world
   the secrets of true joy:

The poor in spirit who embrace
    their ultimate need for God
know they've nothing of themselves—
    God gives them his own kingdom.
And those who mourn their sinfulness
    God comforts and forgives.
To the meek who fight not for the land
    God grants his promised land.
To those who hunger for what is good
    God gives his own good things.
To those who have mercy for all others
    God grants his richest mercy.
The pure of heart who long for good
    find God, eternal Good.
Those who bring God's peace to others
    find God, peace-giving Father.
And those who suffer for what is right
    God receives into his realm.

Jesus ratifies Moses' ten commands
    and teaches the path to God's heart.
From first to last, and last to first,
    God's kingdom is the prize.

Jesus, teacher of deepest truth,
    lead us to our Father's side!

To Suffer for Jesus Is to Be Blessed

Mt 5:11-12: *"Blessed are you when people revile you and persecute you and utter all kinds of evil against you falsely on my account. Rejoice and be glad, for your reward is great in heaven, for in the same way they persecuted the prophets who were before you."*

To contemplate:

The blessing of all blessings best
   has been reserved for everyone
      who suffers for the holy one
         who taught beatitudes.
Matthew's Jesus challenges us:
   "If you really would remain with me,
      then brace yourself to bear with me
         the insults of the world.
"If you would find true happiness,
   fulfillment of your deep desires—
      if you'd forever rejoice with me,
         first endure with me.

"To let me open heaven for you,
    prepare to have earth closed to you—
        to suffer false accusation,
            and even persecution.

"For if you take your stand with me,
    you then become my chosen prophet;
        like every prophet of the past,
            you'll suffer persecution."

Oh, paradoxical reversal!
    Why can the greatest happiness
        be realized only on the road
            of greatest suffering?
Lord, how can you expect a human
    as weak as I to play the hero?
        No hero, but a coward, I.
            How can I be blessed?
Endure injustice, persecution!
    Dear Lord, I can hardly bear
        to think of being ridiculed,
            or unduly criticized.
Does this admission make of me
    one of your chosen "poor in spirit"?
        Help me admit the naked truth:
            without you, I can nothing do!

Be a Light to Others

Mt 5:13-16: *"You are the salt of the earth; but if salt has lost its taste, how can its saltiness be restored? It is no longer good for anything, but is thrown out and trampled under foot. You are the light of the world. A city built on a hill cannot be hid. No one after lighting a lamp puts it under the bushel basket, but on the lampstand, and it gives light to all in the house. In the same way, let your light shine before others, so that they may see your good works and give glory to your Father in heaven."*

To contemplate:

Salt, a light, a city on a hill, a lamp—
  am I to be all these, my Lord?
How can I, who am so utterly tasteless,
  salt society for God's taste?

How can I, who stand in silent darkness,
  brighten other people's way?
How can I become a city on a hill,
  home for the weary wanderer?

How can I become a lamp upon a stand
   shining before others,
   that they may see my good works
   and give glory to my Father?

My good works—my almost non-existent works!
   How will they
   show others the way
   to glory with our Father?

Yet all this you ask of me, my Lord—
   that I give glory to my Father.

I shudder before the task;
   far too much you ask.

Yet I know I have no other choice
   than simply "yes" or "no"—
   you admit no in-between,
   no "maybe" or "perhaps."

Dear Lord, true Light of all the lights,
   I can myself become a light
   only if you are "God-in-me,"
   Salt and Light-in-me.

Keep the Commandments

Mt 5:17-20: *"Do not think that I have come to abolish the law or the prophets; I have come not to abolish but to fulfill. For truly I tell you, until heaven and earth pass away, not one letter, not one stroke of a letter, will pass from the law until all is accomplished. Therefore, whoever breaks one of the least of these commandments, and teaches others to do the same, will be called least in the kingdom of heaven; but whoever does them and teaches them will be called great in the kingdom of heaven. For I tell you, unless your righteousness exceeds that of the scribes and Pharisees, you will never enter the kingdom of heaven."*

To contemplate:

"The law and the prophets"—Scriptures—
   speak of the great Messiah,
     declare his coming,
   tell of his mighty works—
even his most terrible sufferings.

And here you stand upon your mountain,
   telling the whole wide world
      that every letter
  of each and every prophecy
will be fulfilled—achieved in you.
Though sky and earth may disappear,
   God's will you promise to fulfill
      in every last detail,
   commanding us to do the same
if we would enter heaven's reign.
Our righteousness—our goodness—
   will in the end be measured
      by our faithfulness
  in keeping even the least
of God's commandments in our lives.
Do you demand of us, dear Lord,
   that we must always be
      even more faithful
  than scribes and Pharisees,
the Jewish religious leaders of your time?
Can you expect of ordinary folk
   more than of teachers
      of the law,
  under threat of exclusion
  from your Father's house?

O wisest teacher of them all,
   teach me how I too must live—
     I listen, Lord, to you....

Do Not Offend Your Brother or Sister

Mt 5:21-24: *"You have heard that it was said to those of ancient times, 'You shall not murder'; and 'whoever murders shall be liable to judgment.' But I say to you that if you are angry with a brother or sister, you will be liable to judgment; and if you insult a brother or sister, you will be liable to the council; and if you say, 'You fool,' you will be liable to the hell of fire. So when you are offering your gift at the altar, if you remember that your brother or sister has something against you, leave your gift there before the altar and go; first be reconciled to your brother or sister, and then come and offer your gift."*

To contemplate:

Upon the mountain Jesus stands,
　　appealing to the consciences
　　　　of men and women formed in law,
　　　　　　God's law proclaimed by Moses.
"But I say to you," cries Jesus
　　with an authority all his own,
　　　　"Do not be angry with your brother
　　　　　　or give vent to wounding words

or inmost hurting epithets;
        you won't escape God's justice—
to your Father, his children
are more important than your worship."
The fundamental law of nature—
    do not kill another person—
        Jesus deepens and extends
            to include the whole person:
            "Do not kill his human soul,
        his reputation or his honor;
    do not even hurt his feelings
or ruffle up his anger."
Jesus, wisest among all teachers,
    interprets Moses' tenfold law
        in the bright light of God's will—
            he demands we seek our peace
            with all our brothers, sisters,
        before we offer sacrifice
    to seek our peace with God
and worship his creative might.
Jesus, help me embrace our Father's will
    to love my brothers, sisters—all.

Seek Reconciliation Now

Mt 5:25-26: *"Come to terms quickly with your accuser while you are on the way to court with him, or your accuser may hand you over to the judge, and the judge to the guard, and you will be thrown into prison. Truly I tell you, you will never get out until you have paid the last penny."*

To contemplate:

Reconciliation
   is an urgent matter;
     for we are on the way
       to judgment!
We, all of us,
   travel this road together,
     this short road of life
       to our judge.
If on the way
   I hurt a fellow pilgrim,
     owe him great or small
       repayment,

better to make peace
    with him along the way,
        than to arrive at court,
            owing him.
For the great judge
    is not to be trifled with;
        he demands full payment
            of recompense.

O Jesus, why so stern
    a picture of our God?
        Is he not also our own
            dear Father?
Is this your way
    of telling us his will
        that we urgently seek peace
            with one another?
You are in earnest
    that we mend our ways,
        allow no slightest slip
            of vigilance
in our relationship
    with every sister, brother.
        Peaceful Lord, help us live
            in peace with one another!

Adultery Begins in the Heart

Mt 5:27-30: *"You have heard that it was said, 'You shall not commit adultery.' But I say to you that everyone who looks at a woman with lust has already committed adultery with her in his heart. If your right eye causes you to sin, tear it out and throw it away; it is better for you to lose one of your members than for your whole body to be thrown into hell. And if your right hand causes you to sin, cut it off and throw it away; it is better for you to lose one of your members than for your whole body to go into hell."*

To contemplate:

Again Matthew's moral guide proposes
   a deeper interpretation
      of Moses' tenfold law
      and sees adultery
      as more than bodily.
Jesus goes straight to the very heart itself
   as the seat of good or evil,
      distinguishing heart
      of deep respectful love
      from heart of selfish lust.

What terrifying images of eye and hand
   our teacher here evokes—
      tearing out offending eye,
      cutting off transgressing hand,
      throwing body into hell!
Evidence of vehemence
   against adultery,
      even lustful look
      from lustful heart—
      inner source of sin.
Gentle Lord who blessed the poor,
   the humble hearts acknowledging
      their human helplessness,
      their need of holy grace
      to live the kingdom way—
Gentle Lord who blessed the poor,
   how can you demand so much
      of poor human weakness?
      How can you command us
      to control our sensuality?
Only if you truly know the source
   of our inner happiness—
      straightforward heart
      that instead of lusting
      loves!

---

*Mt 5:31-32 = Mk 9:43-47 "Who divorces his wife...causes her to
commit adultery."*

Let Your "Yes" Mean "Yes"

Mt 5:33-37: *"Again, you have heard that it was said to those of ancient times, 'You shall not swear falsely, but carry out the vows you have made to the Lord.' But I say to you, Do not swear at all, either by heaven, for it is the throne of God, or by the earth, for it is his footstool, or by Jerusalem, for it is the city of the great King. And do not swear by your head, for you cannot make one hair white or black. Let your word be 'Yes, Yes' or 'No, No'; anything more than this comes from the evil one."*

To contemplate:

Matthew's great teacher is not content
that we control our anger and our lust.
   More he demands more than moralists
   who quibble about oaths and vows.
He speaks in the highest images
   and the lowest—
images of heaven as God's high throne,
   of earth as his footstool,
of Jerusalem as city of great King,
   of head and single hair.

What control do we have over all these?
   Can we throw down God's throne
      by our broken word?
   Can we raise up God's earth
      by our truthful word?
   Can we even change a single hair
      by what we say or mean?
How then can we invoke such things
   as assurance we speak truth?
Can we presume to think these things
   really anchor our weak words?
"Let your word be
   'Yes,' simply 'Yes,'
   or 'No,' only 'No.'
Don't add embellishments
   that only cloud
   the false or true.
Simplicity's the way
   to make your meaning clear."
O Jesus, master teacher of all truth,
   cleanse my speech
      of vain expressions
   that twist truth into lie,
      or shadow light.

Turn the Other Cheek

Mt 5:38-42: *"You have heard that it was said, 'An eye for an eye and a tooth for a tooth.' But I say to you, Do not resist an evildoer. But if anyone strikes you on the right cheek, turn the other also; and if anyone wants to sue you and take your coat, give your cloak as well; and if anyone forces you to go one mile, go also the second mile. Give to everyone who begs from you, and do not refuse anyone who wants to borrow from you."*

To contemplate:

"Do not resist an evildoer!"
Lord Jesus, what do you expect of us?
"If he strikes you on one cheek,
turn to him the other!"
Lord Jesus, why command of us such gesture?
Not to resist would make us cowards;
To turn the other cheek would make us clowns.
Cowards and clowns—
are these what Christians are?
What did you yourself do
when they struck you on the cheek?

When the guard struck you
for what he thought an arrogant answer
        to the high priest,
    you did not turn the other cheek.
Rather, you challenged him to be a person,
    to act as a thinking man:
    "If I have spoken wrongly,
        tell us what the wrong.
    But if I have spoken rightly,
        why do you strike me?" (Jn 18:23).
Is not your action the best interpretation
        of your spoken word?
    Does "turn the other cheek" then mean
        "Stop the evil cycle
    by challenging the offender
        to think about his act"?

Then I can really "turn the other cheek"
    and not resist an evil-doer,
        without becoming a coward
            or a clown!
But Lord, I can refuse to resist the hurt
    and with you turn the other cheek,
        only if you enfold my cross
            in yours.

Love Your Enemies

Mt 5:43-48: *"You have heard that it was said, 'You shall love your neighbor and hate your enemy.' But I say to you, love your enemies and pray for those who persecute you, so that you may be children of your Father in heaven; for he makes his sun rise on the evil and on the good, and sends rain on the righteous and on the unrighteous. For if you love those who love you, what reward do you have? Do not even the tax collectors do the same? And if you greet only your brothers and sisters, what more are you doing than others? Do not even the Gentiles do the same? Be perfect, therefore, as your heavenly Father is perfect."*

To contemplate:

"Love your enemies;
pray for those who persecute you!"
What human being can understand such folly?
What self-respecting person
can be a doormat?

"Love your enemies!"
How do you expect to win followers
with such a meaningless, self-demeaning demand?
Who will follow you now, Jesus,
into nobodyness?

"Love your enemies!"
O Jesus, you know a different Father
than the God we think we know:
"Your Father in heaven
loves all men and women.
He makes his sun and rain for all of us,
for bad as well as good,
in the perfection of his ways.
If you are really his,
you must be perfect, too!"

O Jesus, God's own Son,
smiling like God's shining sun
upon the poor and weak of all the world,
teaching us, upon the Mount,
your kingdom way.
And am I not, like my enemy, poor and weak?
O Jesus, let your smile shine
on my enemy
and me!

"Pray to Your Father in Secret"

Mt 6:1-6: *"Beware of practicing your piety before others in order to be seen by them; for then you have no reward from your Father in heaven.*

"So whenever you give alms, do not sound a trumpet before you, as the hypocrites do...so that they may be praised by others. Truly I tell you, they have received their reward. But when you give alms, do not let your left hand know what your right hand is doing, so that your alms may be done in secret; and your Father who sees in secret will reward you. And whenever you pray, do not be like the hypocrites; for they love to stand and pray in the synagogues and at the street corners, so that they may be seen by others. Truly I tell you, they have received their reward. But whenever you pray, go into your room and shut the door and pray to your Father who is in secret; and your Father who sees in secret will reward you."

To contemplate:

Jesus, you obviously hate hypocrisy:
    our showing off our piety,
    showing off our giving alms,
    showing off our prayers to God.

Your pictures of hypocrites are graphic:
   sounding trumpet before giving alms,
   praying in public, even on streets
   to attract the praise of others.

"Let not your left hand know
   what your right hand does."
   How extreme your word to tell us,
   "Count not your own good deeds."
"Your Father who dwells in secret
   will so secretly reward you,
   that even you, you yourself,
   will know only after death!"

Jesus, yours are hard words to keep;
   eager as I am for others' praise,
   credit for any good I do,
   reward for every effort.
Jesus, you present me with a choice:
   "Seek praise that men and women give,
   or that which only God can give;
   you cannot have them both!"

Father, I choose your secret way,
   your way of pure sincerity.
   Help me always be true to you,
   and Jesus' way for me.

O God, Our Father!

Mt 6:7-13: *"When you are praying, do not heap up empty phrases as the Gentiles do; for they think that they will be heard because of their many words. Do not be like them, for your Father knows what you need before you ask him.*

"Pray then in this way:
Our Father in heaven,
hallowed be your name.
Your kingdom come.
Your will be done, on earth as it is in heaven."

To contemplate:

"Our Father!" Not even Abraham called you *"Father"!*
Nor Moses nor Elijah nor anyone else
in the same way that Jesus did.
Only Jesus calls you *loving Father*
who knows our every need, even before we ask.

"Our Father in heaven, hallowed be your name."
Not just "Father" or "My Father"
but *"Our* Father."
We are all in this prayer together,
Jesus' followers who believe you are our Father.
"Our Father in heaven"—loving Father who lives
in heaven—whose presence *is* heaven,
right here with us.
And wherever you do not dwell
must be the worst of places—very hell!
"Our Father in heaven, hallowed be your name."
May all men and women call you holy,
the truly holy one.
Heaven is where you are and where we
acknowledge you as the holy, holy, holy one.

"Your kingdom come, come upon this, our earth."
For our earth is not yours now;
we act as if it's ours!
How long before we realize it can
become a place of peace only when it's yours?

"Your will be done, on earth as it is in heaven."
For where your will is really done,
that place is heaven.
Earth will be yours, only yours,
when we do your will, as angels in heaven do.
Your will be done in me!

Give Us What We Need
to Be Your Children

Mt 6:9-13: *"Pray then in this way:*
Our Father in heaven...
Give us this day our daily bread.
And forgive us our debts, as we also have forgiven
our *debtors.*
And do not bring us to the time of trial, but rescue
us *from the evil one."*

To contemplate:

"Give us this day our daily bread"
of wheat, our body-food
for health,
peace and security.
"Give us this day our daily bread,"
the strong sustaining word
your Son,
your Word, relayed to us.

"Give us this day our daily bread,"
the bread of life, your Son,
    our God-with-us
in sacrament he made for us—
"bread" to eat and "wine" to drink
    his body and his blood!

"Forgive our debts, as we forgive"
    the debts that we incur
        by sins—
    sins of mind and heart.
"Forgive our sins, as we forgive
    all those who injure us."
        O Father,
    give us your generosity
to forgive as wholeheartedly as you.

"Father, do not bring us to the trial,"
    lest we fail to keep faith
        with you.
    We are fragile, much too weak
to stand firm and give our lives for you.

"O Father, rescue us from the evil one"—
    from the tempter whom we fear—
        through your Son
    give us his steadfastness;
give us all we need to be your own!

Do Penance Cheerfully

Mt 6:16-18: *"And whenever you fast, do not look dismal, like the hypocrites, for they disfigure their faces so as to show others that they are fasting. Truly I tell you, they have received their reward. But when you fast, put oil on your head and wash your face, so that your fasting may be seen not by others but by your Father who is in secret; and your Father who sees in secret will reward you."*

To contemplate:

Again, my Jesus, you demand
   my undivided heart,
a pure intention in my acts,
   straight arrows to their mark—
   the Father's holy will.
No mixing in of selfishness
   that vitiates my will
and turns the act I offer up
   to my heavenly Father
   back to me for praise.

What fool, the worldly hypocrite
   who puts on gloomy look
and even dirties his face
   to attract our human eyes
   to his fasting for his God.
Yet am I not guilty of such fraud
   when I make an outward show
of being inward what I'm not,
   hiding my true sentiments
   beneath mask of smiling face?
Today we make a different show,
   a pretense of false worth
in clothes we wear or cars we drive
   to impress the world around
   by display of hollow pretense.
How hard to learn your way, dear Lord,
   your noble, simple way
of doing all to praise the Father.
   How easily we frustrate
   giving God the glory!
O teacher of the Father's love,
   O Wisdom of the Father,
teach us to seek the only thing
   that brings us happiness—
   your straight and simple way
   to the heart of our Father-God.

Where Your Treasure Is, There Is Your Heart

Mt 6:19-24: *"Do not store up for yourselves treasures on earth, where moth and rust consume and where thieves break in and steal; but store up for yourselves treasures in heaven, where neither moth nor rust consumes and where thieves do not break in and steal. For where your treasure is, there your heart will be also.*

"The eye is the lamp of the body. So, if your eye is healthy, your whole body will be full of light; but if your eye is unhealthy, your whole body will be full of darkness. If then the light in you is darkness, how great is the darkness! No one can serve two masters; for a slave will either hate the one and love the other, or be devoted to the one and despise the other. You cannot serve God and wealth."

To contemplate:

In your presence, Lord, I ask myself:
Where does my treasure lie?
Does my heart yearn for this world's goods
more than for your grace?
Do I love my house, my car, my clothes,
my gadgets and my things

more than I long to be with you
    in your Father's house?
What does my eye most often seek—
    the beauty of this world,
or the inner light that warms my heart
    with the love you love to give?
Is the inner eye of my own heart
    blinded by outer sight
of things forbidden by your word—
    displays that raise my lust?
Is the inner eye of my own heart
    clouded by outer sight
of things that pass in the dark night
    of our poor, passing world?

Ah, Lord, you challenge all of us
    to look within our hearts
and break the ties that weaken them
    and tear our ties to you.
You challenge us to break the bonds
    that steal our hearts from you.
You won't abide a rivalry
    between yours and another's love.
A heart divided between two lords,
    you will not tolerate.
Then take my heart, my Lord!

Your Father Loves You!

Mt 6:25-26: *"I tell you, do not worry about your life, what you will eat or what you will drink, or about your body, what you will wear. Is not life more than food, and the body more than clothing? Look at the birds of the air; they neither sow nor reap nor gather into barns, and yet your heavenly Father feeds them. Are you not of more value than they?"*

To contemplate:

"Look at the birds of the air!"
    My Lord, have I ever really seen
        the birds of the air?
I look but do not see the birds—
    oh yes, I see them fly and flit;
        I see them feed.
But I seldom see them in the light
    of our sweet Father's love,
        his care for them.

And how seldom do I see myself
    in light of my Father's love,
        his care for me.

I labor and sweat to feed and clothe
   the body his love gives me—
     and forget him.
The birds don't worry what to eat
   or what to wear or anything.
     They're free as birds!

But I have little freedom to think
   of my Father's greater love—
     I'm a slave to things.
If he loves the little birds so much
   and takes good care of them,
     why not of me?

O Jesus, open wide my eyes to see
   the birds my Father loves—
     he loves me more!

Father, into your loving hands
   I entrust my past and future—
     I trust in you.
For the Son that you have given me
   is God-who-lives-in-me—
     and I-in-him!

Your Father Cares for You

Mt 6:27-34: *"Can any of you by worrying add a single hour to your span of life? Why do you worry about clothing? Consider the lilies of the field...they neither toil nor spin, yet I tell you, even Solomon in all his glory was not clothed like one of these. But if God so clothes the grass of the field, which is alive today and tomorrow is thrown into the oven, will he not much more clothe you—you of little faith? Therefore do not worry, saying, 'What will we eat?' or 'What will we drink?' or 'What will we wear?' For it is the Gentiles who strive for all these things; and indeed your heavenly Father knows that you need all these things. But strive first for the kingdom of God and his righteousness, and all these things will be given to you as well.*

"So do not worry about tomorrow, for tomorrow will bring worries of its own. Today's trouble is enough for today."

To contemplate:

"Can worrying add a single hour to your life?"
  Lord, you ask such challenging questions.

Add to life? My worrying *shortens* my life;
    yet I keep on worrying—a chronic worrier, I.
You point to the wild flowers of the field,
    wild flowers I seldom see,
        never see as clothed by God—
            oh, what a God have we!
How long since I've really looked at grass,
    a single beautiful blade of grass
        that lasts so short a time,
            yet is adorned by God.

"You of little faith," you say to me;
    and I can only nod in shame,
        admitting the truth you speak;
            I have so little faith!
"Strive first for God's goodly kingdom."
    Your word pierces my thick armor.
        What defense can I erect
            against clear truth?
"Today's trouble is enough for today."
    So why do I worry about tomorrow?
        If God cares for me today,
            will he not, tomorrow?

O Jesus, greatest teacher of them all,
    thanks for your reflections deep;
        you teach me that our caring God
            is my own *Father-God!*

Clear Your Own Sight First

Mt 7:1-5: *"Do not judge, so that you may not be judged. For with the judgment you make you will be judged, and the measure you give will be the measure you get. Why do you see the speck in your neighbor's eye, but do not notice the log in your own eye? Or how can you say to your neighbor, 'Let me take the speck out of your eye,' while the log is in your own eye? You hypocrite, first take the log out of your own eye, and then you will see clearly to take the speck out of your neighbor's eye."*

To contemplate:

Once more your word is like a two-edged sword,
   cutting through my crooked conscience,
     baring the double standard
  by which I sharply judge all others,
yet blandly excuse the same faults in myself.
How critical I am of all my brothers, sisters,
   expecting perfection of their acts,
     permitting myself much less!
  With the measure I begrudge to them,
our God, you testify, will measure out to me.

How miserly I measure out my gifts to them.
How eagerly I long for gifts to me.
Again the double standard
you reveal in me with two-edged sword
that cuts through every screen I can devise.
I find myself looking at the world around me
and wondering why so many people
can be so evil-minded.
Only your sword-sharp word to me
can open up my hidden depths of arrogance.
As you have said, I do not see objectively—
that log lodged there within my eye
blocks my view of others,
lets me only inward look, not outward,
lest I see more good in others than in myself.

Lord, must I, then, reform myself
before I can another help?
How can I see the obstacle
in my own eye, and so pluck it out?
I can't! Dear Lord, please
stoop down to me,
lovingly;
pluck out that log,
that my eye may truly see!

Ask, and Your Father Will Respond

Mt 7:6-11: *"Do not give what is holy to dogs; and do not throw your pearls before swine, or they will trample them under foot and turn and maul you.*

"Ask, and it will be given you; search, and you will find; knock, and the door will be opened for you. For everyone who asks receives, and everyone who searches finds, and for everyone who knocks, the door will be opened. Is there anyone among you who, if your child asks for bread, will give a stone? Or if the child asks for a fish, will give a snake? If you then, who are evil, know how to give good gifts to your children, how much more will your Father in heaven give good things to those who ask him!"

To contemplate:

You tell me not to waste your gospel pearl
    on unbelieving swine;
yet you offer even me your precious pearl,
    to me of little faith.
O let me trample not with careless foot
    the pearl you offer me.

Your pearl is truth that God, my Father dear,
    holds out to me as gift,
just for my asking him as his small child,
    who places trust in him.
For little child who truly trusts his father,
    asks all with certainty.
The proof of faith, then, is in the asking,
    the knocking at his door.
The evidence of faith is in the seeking,
    the seeking for always more
from my good Father who dwells in heaven,
    awaiting my trusting call.
O Jesus, you challenge me to deeper faith,
    a faith that leads to prayer
of complete, unwavering confidence in the God
    who knows before I ask
my needs so deep that I myself don't know,
    or even dare to ask.
Yet dare I must to show I trust in him,
    dare ask for anything!
For miracles of grace and truest love,
    for simple things of earth,
believing with my heart and soul
    he'll give me what I need.

Then, Father dear, I ask, I knock—
    I seek to love your Son!

The Gate Is Narrow

Mt 7:12-20: *"In everything do to others as you would have them do to you; for this is the law and the prophets.*

"Enter through the narrow gate; for the gate is wide and the road is easy that leads to destruction, and there are many who take it. For the gate is narrow and the road is hard that leads to life, and there are few who find it.

"Beware of false prophets, who come to you in sheep's clothing but inwardly are ravenous wolves. You will know them by their fruits. Are grapes gathered from thorns, or figs from thistles? In the same way, every good tree bears good fruit, but the bad tree bears bad fruit. A good tree cannot bear bad fruit, nor can a bad tree bear good fruit. Every tree that does not bear good fruit is cut down and thrown into the fire. Thus you will know them by their fruits."

To contemplate:

If it is your law, my Lord,
  that I treat others as I
    expect them to treat me,

then the gate is truly narrow
    that opens to your kingdom.
        How can I enter in?

If the road is so hard, Lord,
    that leads toward life in you,
        how can I walk upon it?
If along that road I meet "sheep"
    that are really ravenous wolves,
        how can I survive them?

If by my fruits, my mature acts,
    you judge me good or evil, Lord,
        you will not tolerate my faults.
Your words sound harsh to me,
    too sharp with stern demand.
        How can I be saved?

Only if you hear my cry, dear Lord,
    as I ask to walk your road with you—
        only then, my Lord.
Only if you open up your narrow gate
    to my persistent knock—
        only then, my Lord.

Only if you cultivate my roots,
    make good fruit grow in me—
        only then, my Lord.

Build on Rock

Mt 7:21-29: *"Not everyone who says to me, 'Lord, Lord,' will enter the kingdom of heaven, but only the one who does the will of my Father in heaven. On that day many will say to me, 'Lord, Lord, did we not prophesy in your name, and cast out demons in your name, and do many deeds of power in your name?' Then I will declare to them, 'I never knew you; go away from me, you evildoers.'*

"Everyone then who hears these words of mine and acts on them will be like a wise man who built his house on rock. The rain fell, the floods came, and the winds blew and beat on that house, but it did not fall, because it had been founded on rock. And everyone who hears these words of mine and does not act on them will be like a foolish man who built his house on sand. The rain fell, and the floods came, and the winds blew and beat against that house, and it fell—and great was its fall!"

Now when Jesus had finished saying these things, the crowds were astounded at his teaching, for he taught them as one having authority....

To contemplate:

Deeds rather than words convince you, Lord,
    deeds that fulfill your Father's will.

O Lord, I have been calling you *"my* Lord,"
    but not as empty word of wind, I hope.

Yet empty deeds like empty words, you say,
    will fail to open the narrow gate.
Not prophecy, not casting out demons;
    not even miracles can open that gate.

No word or work of mine can heaven gain;
    only you, my Lord, can open it to me.

My Lord, you are the rock on which I build—
    you, the rock on which I build my life!
Your word stands firmer than polished granite;
    no wind or rain can undermine it.

On this unyielding rock I build my life
    to share your firm, unwavering strength.
For you alone speak words of God,
    you alone are the Father's very Word.

Not my word, Lord, but yours the word I trust;
    not my work, Lord; yours the work that saves.
For I believe in your authority, my Lord.
    Oh, guide me to our Father's side!

Mt 8:1-4 = Mk 1:40-44 Jesus cures a leper.

Lord, I Am Not Worthy!

Mt 8:5-13: *When he entered Capernaum, a centurion came to him, appealing to him and saying, "Lord, my servant is lying at home paralyzed, in terrible distress." And he said to him, "I will come and cure him." The centurion answered, "Lord, I am not worthy to have you come under my roof; but only speak the word, and my servant will be healed. For I also am a man under authority, with soldiers under me; and I say to one, 'Go,' and he goes, and to another, 'Come,' and he comes, and to my slave, 'Do this,' and the slave does it." When Jesus heard him, he was amazed and said to those who followed him, "Truly I tell you, in no one in Israel have I found such faith. I tell you, many will come from east and west and will eat with Abraham and Isaac and Jacob in the kingdom of heaven, while the heirs of the kingdom will be thrown into the outer darkness, where there will be weeping and gnashing of teeth." And to the centurion Jesus said, "Go; let it be done for you according to your faith." And the servant was healed in that hour.*

To contemplate:

Here, a great healing to confirm your word
    as authority claiming our belief.
        "Lord, I am not worthy
to have you come under my roof"—
I, too, would speak this humble word.

For this is the word that wins your heart,
    word of faith in your control
        of even body-health.
    Your offer to go to a sick slave
draws the deep response of a soldier's faith.

His faith, so profound it amazes you,
    wins surprisingly great praise
        and miraculous act,
    and prophecy that seeming outsiders
may enter God's kingdom before his chosen ones.

For only you, Lord, can swing the narrow gate
    open for us pleading pilgrims,
        open for our faith.
    The alternative you paint for us
in dark images of sobs and gnashing teeth.

Oh, then, my Lord, increase my faith
    that I may hear you say to me,
"Let it be done likewise for you
    according to your faith!"

Mt 8:14-15 = Mk 1:30-31 Jesus cures Peter's mother-in-law.

He Bore Our Infirmities

Mt 8:16-22: *That evening they brought to him many who were possessed with demons; and he cast out the spirits with a word, and cured all who were sick. This was to fulfill what had been spoken through the prophet Isaiah, "He took our infirmities and bore our diseases."*

Now when Jesus saw great crowds around him, he gave orders to go over to the other side. A scribe then approached and said, "Teacher, I will follow you wherever you go." And Jesus said to him, "Foxes have holes, and birds of the air have nests; but the Son of Man has nowhere to lay his head." Another of his disciples said to him, "Lord, first let me go and bury my father." But Jesus said to him, "Follow me, and let the dead bury their own dead."

To contemplate:

You cured "all who were sick";
   not one did you leave unhealed.
How could you cure them all, my Lord—
   how cure every one?
Only by taking upon yourself
   the diseases they brought to you,

holding in compassionate heart
    the burdens of them all.

You are, indeed, the Son of Man,
    vulnerable like me;
a man who suffers along with us,
    suffers all our ills.
A wandering Son of Man are you,
    without a home or bed—
a homeless pilgrim on the earth,
    sharing our rootlessness.

A learned scribe who sees you're wise
    calls you "teacher"; he would follow.
You warn him sharply he must lose
    even home to follow you.
A disciple who sees more deeply yet,
    calls you "Lord"; he'd follow too.
You warn him with seeming cruel word:
    "Let the dead bury their dead."

Are you saying, Lord, that they are dead
    who neglect their living kin?
Lord, give me your compassionate heart
    to love the human family
      enough to follow you!

Lord, Save Us!

Mt 8:23-27: *And when he got into the boat, his disciples followed him. A windstorm arose on the sea, so great that the boat was being swamped by the waves; but he was asleep. And they went and woke him up, saying, "Lord, save us! We are perishing!" And he said to them, "Why are you afraid, you of little faith?" Then he got up and rebuked the winds and the sea; and there was a dead calm. They were amazed, saying, "What sort of man is this, that even the winds and the sea obey him?"*

To contemplate:

Jesus has just warned two would-be followers
   of the perils of following him:
     the homelessness,
   even giving up family.
Yet into a fragile boat disciples follow him.
Jesus, why do you sleep as a storm blows up—
   to test your disciples' faith?
     No, you are spent
   from long hours of ministry.
You are true man who suffers even our fatigue.
They come to you: "Lord, save us, or we perish!"

They believe that you and only you
    can save them now.
Yet you ask them why they fear
and chastise them as men of "little faith."
Too little faith! Lord, what do you expect?
    That we relax in our Father's arms
        even as you did?
    Relax in the midst of stormy sea,
our raging sea of modern stress-driven lives?
We do relax as we contemplate your saving act,
    standing in the storm-tossed boat,
        calming wind and sea!
    Yes, we need not fear the storm;
Lord, we can relax if you are in our boat.
Give us the tranquil peace in which you rested
    in your Father's omnipotent arms—
        even through our storms.
    Amaze us as your true disciples,
who see you as the Son of Man, yet Son of God.
And when our boat of life seems swamped by
    waves,
    remind us of your presence here
        within our hearts,
    and rise up once more, dear Lord,
to rescue us and bring us to our Father's arms.

*Mt 8:28-34 = Mk 4:35-5:17; Mt 9:1-15 = Mk 2:3-20 Jesus heals the
Gadarene demoniacs and a paralytic, calls Matthew, and responds to
a question about fasting.*

New Wine in New Wineskins

Mt 9:16-17: *"No one sews a piece of unshrunk cloth on an old cloak, for the patch pulls away from the cloak, and a worse tear is made. Neither is new wine put into old wineskins; otherwise, the skins burst, and the wine is spilled, and the skins are destroyed; but new wine is put into fresh wineskins, and so both are preserved."*

To contemplate:

Jesus is such a master of metaphor;
   he makes us think and wonder:

Why not use new cloth to patch the old?
   After one washing you will see!
The new cloth, not preshrunk in Jesus' day,
   will pull away, causing a greater tear.
Why not use old wineskins for new wine?
   In a short time you will see!
New wine, still fermenting, will expand
   and burst through old brittle skins.
But what, Lord, what is the significance
   of homespun metaphors like these?

Are you referring to your teaching as so new
    it breaks the forms your hearers give it?
But your new revelation stretches beyond,
    just as your actions rise above
all the people's expectations,
    and your life exceeds all bounds.
Unpredictable, even though predicted,
    you live your life not by human rules,
but by the mysterious plan of your Father-God.
    Your cloth, dear Lord, entirely new,
    breaks right through the threads of older kinds;
Your wine is so much stronger drink
    no man or woman can lightly take it down.

O Lord, thanks for new wineskins and new cloth—
    new forms of your newly founded Church,
your Church with all its sacraments of grace
    your gifts down all the years to us!

Mt 9:18-26 = Mk 5:22-43 Jesus heals a woman of hemorrhages and restores a girl to life.

Jesus Heals the Blind

Mt 9:27-31: *As Jesus went on from there, two blind men followed him, crying loudly, "Have mercy on us, Son of David!" When he entered the house, the blind men came to him; and Jesus said to them, "Do you believe that I am able to do this?" They said to him, "Yes, Lord." Then he touched their eyes and said, "According to your faith let it be done to you." And their eyes were opened. Then Jesus sternly ordered them, "See that no one knows of this." But they went away and spread the news about him throughout that district.*

To contemplate:

"Have mercy on us, Son of David!
    We are blind, we cannot see;
        we stumble and we fall.
"Have mercy on us, Son of David,
    for we are blind in spirit;
        we blunder and we sin.
"Have mercy on us, Son of David,
    for you are our great king;
        you show us how to live."

"Do you believe that I can heal you,
  give you back your inner sight,
    show you the way to life?"

"Yes, Lord, we do believe in you,
  believe in your great power
    to lighten up our life."

Then he touched their eyes and said,
  "As you believe, it's done to you;
    see to it no one knows."
And what was darkness until then
  has become the brightest light,
    the light of Jesus' face—
the face of God out of the black,
  a face so full of kindly light,
    they blink in disbelief.
How can they let no one know
  so great a work as this,
    a moment of such bliss?

To see the face of Jesus shine
  out of our darkest night—
    that will heaven be!

Jesus Heals the Mute

Mt 9:32-38: *After they had gone away, a demoniac who was mute was brought to him. And when the demon had been cast out, the one who had been mute spoke; and the crowds were amazed and said, "Never has anything like this been seen in Israel." But the Pharisees said, "By the ruler of the demons he casts out the demons."*

Then Jesus went about all the cities and villages, teaching in their synagogues, and proclaiming the good news of the kingdom, and curing every disease and every sickness. When he saw the crowds, he had compassion for them, because they were harassed and helpless, like sheep without a shepherd. Then he said to his disciples, "The harvest is plentiful, but the laborers are few; therefore ask the Lord of the harvest to send out laborers into his harvest."

To contemplate:

Out of the deepest silence,
  a silence deep and dark,
the deaf-mute hears a voice—
  strongest in all the world,
    the voice of Jesus Christ.

His voice breaks the silence,
    commands the demon out;
his voice brings peace at last,
    peace where there was none—
        the peace of Jesus Christ.

Two responses to his act:
    the people's, "What a miracle!";
the Pharisees', "What a scam—
    this pretender to be God's son,
        is really Satan's son!"
But Jesus, undeterred by praise,
    or criticism,
goes forth to all the world
    to bring good news of kingdom come,
        the healing of all woes.
The caring, loving shepherd, he,
    of sheep without a guide;
his deep compassion for them all
    reaches out to every one,
        to heal and teach and save.

Good shepherd of all souls is he,
    eager to bring us in
to his Father's harvest feast.
    O Father, Lord of the harvest feast
        thanks for our Good Shepherd!

Mt 10:1-4 = Mk 13-19 Jesus gives some of his authority to the twelve.

Jesus Teaches How to Teach

Mt 10:5-15: *These twelve Jesus sent out with the following instructions: "Go nowhere among the Gentiles, and enter no town of the Samaritans, but go rather to the lost sheep of the house of Israel. As you go, proclaim the good news, 'The kingdom of heaven has come near.' Cure the sick, raise the dead, cleanse the lepers, cast out demons. You received without payment; give without payment. Take no gold, or silver, or copper in your belts, no bag for your journey, or two tunics, or sandals, or a staff; for laborers deserve their food. Whatever town or village you enter, find out who in it is worthy, and stay there until you leave. As you enter the house, greet it. If the house is worthy, let your peace come upon it; but if it is not worthy, let your peace return to you. If anyone will not welcome you or listen to your words, shake off the dust from your feet as you leave that house or town. Truly I tell you, it will be more tolerable for the land of Sodom and Gomorrah on the day of judgment than for that town."*

To contemplate:

"Go to the lost sheep of the house of Israel.
　And as you go, proclaim good news,
　　'Heaven's kingdom has come near.'"
　"To the lost sheep"—
　　Lord, your words are clear.
　　　I, too, am a lost sheep,
　　　　lost without you.

"Cure the sick, raise the dead, cleanse the lepers,
　cast out demons; take no gold or silver,
　　no bag for your journey, no food."
　Lord, your directives
　　are too severe for us.
　　　When we go on a trip,
　　　　we take everything.

Is my house worthy of your peace,
　the peace your envoys offer us?
　　Is mine the kind of house you'd choose
　　　to stay in, rest with me?

Or would you shake its dust from underfoot
　in sign of my unworthiness to hear
　　your word of everlasting peace,
　　　your saving word for me?

Dear Lord, I open wide my door,
　door of my heart to you,
　　my God-with-me!

The Spirit Speaks through You

Mt 10:16-25: *"See, I am sending you out like sheep into the midst of wolves; so be wise as serpents and innocent as doves. Beware of them, for they will hand you over to councils and flog you in their synagogues; and you will be dragged before governors and kings because of me, as a testimony to them and the Gentiles. When they hand you over, do not worry about how you are to speak or what you are to say; for what you are to say will be given to you at that time; for it is not you who speak, but the Spirit of your Father speaking through you. Brother will betray brother to death, and a father his child, and children will rise against parents and have them put to death; and you will be hated by all because of my name. But the one who endures to the end will be saved. When they persecute you in one town, flee to the next; for truly I tell you, you will not have gone through all the towns of Israel before the Son of Man comes.*

"A disciple is not above the teacher, nor a slave above the master; it is enough for the disciple to be like the teacher, and the slave like the master...."

To contemplate:

You send us like sheep into the pack of wolves,
  and tell us to be wise as serpents,
    yet innocent as doves.
  Lord, how do you expect us to survive?
How do you expect us to change wolves into sheep?
Not of ourselves—you don't expect us of ourselves
  to show your gentleness to predators,
    your love to unbelievers.
  Your Spirit alone can speak through us,
the Holy Spirit of your all-holy, loving Father.

O Spirit sent by Jesus and the Father of us all,
  sweet Spirit of the Father's love for us,
    wise Spirit, speak for me!
  In the wolf-pack of this world of ours
where brother turns on brother, father on his child,
I know not how to speak in the cause of Jesus Christ,
  or in my own defense, as his meek dove.
    Wise Spirit, speak for me!
  Speak in my gentle, humble way of life,
Speak in my return of love for hate, to heal the hurt.

Even as you, my Jesus, even as you have done,
  in the Spirit of your loving Father,
    even as you—may I do.
  It is enough that I, your sheep,
become like you, my gentle, loving teacher—
    become like you, God's Lamb (Jn 1:29).

Your Father Counts the Hairs of Your Head

Mt 10:26-33: *"So have no fear of them; for nothing is covered up that will not be uncovered, and nothing secret that will not become known. What I say to you in the dark, tell in the light; and what you hear whispered, proclaim from the housetops. Do not fear those who kill the body but cannot kill the soul; rather fear him who can destroy both soul and body in hell. Are not two sparrows sold for a penny? Yet not one of them will fall to the ground apart from your Father. And even the hairs of your head are all counted. So do not be afraid; you are of more value than many sparrows.*

"Everyone therefore who acknowledges me before others, I also will acknowledge before my Father in heaven; but whoever denies me before others, I also will deny before my Father in heaven."

To contemplate:

"Everything you cover, God will uncover;
    your every secret he'll reveal!"
My God, is there nothing I can hide,
    nothing I can keep from you?

Those deepest secrets of mind and heart,
    more than half-hidden from myself,
cobwebbed over in darkest corner,
    you'll let the whole world know?

O God of openness and truth,
    I fear the bright light of your gaze.
O Jesus, bright light of the Father,
    I fear your piercing sight.
Yet, you tell me not to fear,
    assure me of your Father's love—
a love that even counts my hairs
    and guards them, every one.

I picture you, my Father dear,
    as I comb my thinning hair:
"There goes another, Father dear!
    You've counted that one, too?"
My God, you know my secrets all,
    yet you love my every hair;
I place my utter trust in you
    to love and guard my life.

For I believe your own dear Son,
    acknowledge him to all,
confident he will acknowledge me
    to you, my Father dear!

Whoever Welcomes You
Welcomes Me

Mt 10:34-42: *"Do not think that I have come to bring peace to the earth; I have not come to bring peace, but a sword.*

For I have come to set a man against his father,
and a daughter against her mother...
and one's foes will be members of one's own house
hold.

Whoever loves father or mother more than me is not worthy of me; and whoever loves son or daughter more than me is not worthy of me; and whoever does not take up the cross and follow me is not worthy of me. Those who find their life will lose it, and those who lose their life for my sake will find it.

"Whoever welcomes you welcomes me, and whoever welcomes me welcomes the one who sent me. Whoever welcomes a prophet in the name of a prophet will receive a prophet's reward; and whoever welcomes a righteous person in the name of a righteous person will receive the reward of the righteous; and whoever gives even a cup of cold water to one of these little ones in the name of a disciple—truly I tell you, none of these will lose their reward."

To contemplate:

Jesus, you accept no rival for our love:
   "Whoever loves father or mother
      more than me
         is unworthy of me."
You have brought a sword into our world
   to divide those who love you
      from those who divide their love
         between you and others.
You divide us among ourselves;
   yet you will not let us
      divide our loving hearts
         between you and others!

Why do you tease us with your paradoxes:
   "Those who find life will lose it;
      those who lose their life
         will find it"?
Is it to challenge our love for you,
   dare us welcome you into our lives,
      love you more than all else,
         take up our cross with you?
You challenge us to welcome you,
   welcome you in all our friends,
      welcome you in those in need
         of even a drink of water.
O Jesus, I welcome you into my life.
   Come, drink my cup with me!

Jesus Is the Promised One

Mt 11:2-6: *When John heard in prison what the Messiah was doing, he sent word by his disciples and said to him, "Are you the one who is to come, or are we to wait for another?" Jesus answered them, "Go and tell John what you hear and see: the blind receive their sight, the lame walk, the lepers are cleansed, the deaf hear, the dead are raised, and the poor have good news brought to them. And blessed is anyone who takes no offense at me."*

To contemplate:

Does John have second thoughts
   about who this Jesus is?
      He demands no strict fasts
      and even eats with sinners.
   No justice-dealing ax
lays he to evil roots.
He wields no winnowing fork,
   dividing honest wheat
      from worthless chaff.
      He brings no fierce fire
   from heaven to annihilate
the wicked with God's ire.

Instead he comes in love:
  he gives the blind new sight,
    the lame he prompts to walk;
    the lepers' sores he heals;
  the deaf he helps to hear;
the dead he raises up!
None but good news he brings;
  none but the poor he helps;
    none but the lame, the blind,
    the sick, the lost, the dead—
  only to these he ministers,
only for these he comes.
O Jesus, we are blind and deaf:
  we look but do not see the light;
    we hear but do not understand.
      O Jesus, come again for us
  and lift us from our withered life
into your dynamic good-news life.
O saving Lord, save even us
  from emptiness of sin,
    dark night of separation
    from our loving Father-God.
  Come, live and love in us,
Jesus, our saving God-with-us.

More Than a Prophet

Mt 11:7-15: *As they went away, Jesus began to speak to the crowds about John: "What did you go out into the wilderness to look at? A reed shaken by the wind? What then did you go out to see? Someone dressed in soft robes? Look, those who wear soft robes are in royal palaces. What then did you go out to see? A prophet? Yes, I tell you, and more than a prophet. This is the one about whom it is written,*

'See, I am sending my messenger ahead of you,
who will prepare your way before you.'

Truly I tell you, among those born of women no one has arisen greater than John the Baptist; yet the least in the kingdom of heaven is greater than he. From the days of John the Baptist until now the kingdom of heaven has suffered violence, and the violent take it by force. For all the prophets and the law prophesied until John came; and if you are willing to accept it, he is Elijah who is to come. Let anyone with ears listen!"

To contemplate:

John the Baptist was no weak reed shaken by wind,
    no dandy dressed in delicate robes.
John was a wilderness man, wild and strong,
    dressed in camel's hair and belt,
        a man of piercing look
            and stinging speech.

John was a soul-searching prophet of truth,
    the naked truth of widespread sin.
John was more than prophet, a messenger he,
    a messenger to prepare the way
        for the Savior of the world;
            greater than others, John.

Yet even he knew little of heaven's kingdom,
    the kingdom Jesus has come to bring.
Like Elijah of old, John denounced without fear
    the sinful act of a violent king,
        who'd take heaven by storm
            if only he could.

But John has now fallen victim to the violent king,
    imprisoned by a petty, furious man.
Heaven is not a prize the violent can win;
    the meekest person, poor in spirit,
        is greater than a violent king.
            The kingdom of heaven,
            far beyond our human grasp—
is your gracious gift, O saving Lord!

Jesus, a "Glutton and a Drunkard"

Mt 11:16-19: *"But to what will I compare this generation? It is like children sitting in the marketplaces and
calling to one another,*
> *'We played the flute for you, and you did not dance;*
>   *we wailed, and you did not mourn.'*
*For John came neither eating nor drinking, and they say,
'He has a demon'; the Son of Man came eating and
drinking, and they say, 'Look, a glutton and a drunkard,
a friend of tax collectors and sinners!' Yet wisdom is
vindicated by her deeds."*

To contemplate:

Dear Lord, are we today like those
   you compare to wayward children
who could not choose between two good ways,
   though one was better far?
John preached the way of austerity:
   "Renounce all worldly things,
in hope of winning by severity
   forgiveness of your sins."

You preach a gentle, cheerful way:
    "Embrace your Father's gifts,
in hope of receiving through faith and love
    forgiveness for your sins."
John gave up good food and drink
    for locusts and wild honey,
and people said he was possessed
    by a mad and wicked demon.
You celebrated with repentant
    tax collectors and sinners,
and people labeled you a glutton
    and a worthless drunkard.

Truth will tell the wiser way—
    John's way of deprivation,
or your way of joyful celebration
    of all our Father's gifts.
Truth will tell by deeds of those
    harsh upon themselves;
or joyful toward brothers, sisters,
    for all our Father's gifts.

O gentle Lord, open wide my heart
    to our Father's every child,
that I may live as you have lived—
    with you within my heart.

Repent!

Mt 11:20-24: *Then he began to reproach the cities in which most of his deeds of power had been done, because they did not repent. "Woe to you, Chorazin! Woe to you, Bethsaida! For if the deeds of power done in you had been done in Tyre and Sidon, they would have repented long ago in sackcloth and ashes. But I tell you, on the day of judgment it will be more tolerable for Tyre and Sidon than for you. And you, Capernaum,*
    will you be exalted to heaven?
    No, you will be brought down to Hades.
For if the deeds of power done in you had been done in Sodom, it would have remained until this day. But I tell you that on the day of judgment it will be more tolerable for the land of Sodom than for you."

To contemplate:

Though you tone down John's severity,
    you become severe yourself,
        condemning those who fail to hear
           and repent their sins in fear.

You pronounce that dreadful word of "woe,"
    Prophetic word of doom,
        on all the towns that saw your days,
            yet failed to change their ways.
The towns stern prophet Joel condemned,
    pagan Sidon and ancient Tyre (Joel 4:4),
        and towns that God destroyed in fire,
            old Sodom and Gomorrah—
these towns will have suffered less
    than those that saw your mighty deeds:
        Bethsaida and Capernaum
            have ignored your saving word.
No game is this of careless children
    in the world's wide marketplace;
        you, God's Son, bring rarest gift
            that we may not reject.

People who hope in themselves alone
    burn and sink in hopelessness,
        the world's indifferent men and women,
            ignore the Lord's Anointed One—
                ignore the Lord himself.
O Jesus, have mercy on us all!
    We fail to understand your words
        or the meaning of your deeds.
            We die unless you stoop to us,
                forgiving God-with-us.

"No One Knows the Father Except the Son"

Mt 11:25-27: *At that time Jesus said, "I thank you, Father, Lord of heaven and earth, because you have hidden these things from the wise and the intelligent and have revealed them to infants; yes, Father, for such was your gracious will. All things have been handed over to me by my Father; and no one knows the Son except the Father, and no one knows the Father except the Son and anyone to whom the Son chooses to reveal him."*

To contemplate:

O Father, Lord of heaven and earth,
    thanks for your revelation
of your very self in the gentle Son
    you sent to us little ones.
The great ones are too self-important
    to notice a Jewish teacher
who calls God "Father" and claims to know
    his loving will for us.

What a marvel Jesus opens to us:
    the great Creator of our world,

Lord of earth and the universe,
  is our loving Father-God!
I beg to be one of those little ones
  that Jesus praises here,
not one of the self-important ones
  so "wise" in their own eyes.

O Jesus, only Son of God,
  May I be one of your little ones,
wise enough to realize
  that you are really the only one
who knows who I truly am—
  a beloved child of God!

O Jesus, only Son of God,
  I believe you show your Father
and his loving will for us
  in your every word and act.
I believe your Father has given you
  authority to speak for him
and do all in his behalf,
  to save us from ourselves.

Lord Jesus, I believe in you,
  our saving "God-with-us!"

"Come to Me!"

Mt 11:28-30: *"Come to me, all you that are weary and are carrying heavy burdens, and I will give you rest. Take my yoke upon you, and learn from me; for I am gentle and humble in heart, and you will find rest for your souls. For my yoke is easy, and my burden is light."*

To contemplate:

Yes, Lord, I'm very weary
   of my heavy burden
      of selfishness
         and sin.
O gentle heart of gentle Lord,
   O humble heart of God!
      Grant me your rest,
         soul-rest.
O humble heart of humble God,
   Jesus, Son of God;
      your heart is heart
         of God!

If I can love your human heart,
I love the heart of God.
If I can love *you*,
I love God.
The yoke we put upon ourselves
is a heavy yoke, indeed.
But *your* load is light
and easy.
The burden of sin we try to bear
is a heavy burden, Lord.
But you carry it
for us.

Gentle Jesus, my humble Lord,
let me gentle, humble be,
faithful image
of you.
Gentle in action, humble in word—
that is you, my Lord.
Make me gentle,
too.

Then, Lord, my Father's truest Son,
I'll be conformed to you,
my gentle, humble
God-with-me.

Mt 12:1-14 = Mk 2:23-3:6 Jesus is Son of Man and Lord of the sabbath.

Here Is My Servant

Mt 12:15-23: *When Jesus became aware of this [the plot of the Pharisees to kill him], he departed. Many crowds followed him, and he cured all of them, and he ordered them not to make him known. This was to fulfill what had been spoken through the prophet Isaiah:*

"Here is my servant, whom I have chosen,
  my beloved, with whom my soul is well pleased.
I will put my Spirit upon him,
  and he will proclaim justice to the Gentiles.
He will not wrangle or cry aloud,
  nor will anyone hear his voice in the streets.
He will not break a bruised reed
  or quench a smoldering wick
until he brings justice to victory.
  And in his name the Gentiles will hope."

Then they brought to him a demoniac who was blind and mute; and he cured him, so that the one who had been mute could speak and see. All the crowds were amazed and said, "Can this be the Son of David?"

To contemplate:

Centuries ago, Isaiah wrote
  of a servant God would send
  and anoint with his Holy Spirit.
To Gentiles he would send his herald
  to proclaim justice, peace.
Gentle and kind would this servant be,
  to all the broken-hearted—
  bruised reeds and smoldering wicks.

Jesus, Isaiah's promised one,
  up-braces the bruised reed,
  rekindles fire in smoldering wick.
He reaches out to lame and blind,
  curing all their ills,
  yet bids them not to make him known.
Hope to the hopeless, joy to the joyless,
  he fulfills their every need,
  casts out blinding, deafening demon.

The crowd recalls Isaiah's promise,
  "Can this be David's Son?"
Yes, you are David's Son and more:
  You are our God-with-us!

Mt 12:24-32 = Mk 3:22-30 Jesus refutes the charge that he works by Beelzebul.

Out of the Heart the Mouth Speaks

Mt 12:33-37: [Jesus said to the Pharisees,] "Either make the tree good, and its fruit good; or make the tree bad, and its fruit bad; for the tree is known by its fruit. You brood of vipers! How can you speak good things, when you are evil? For out of the abundance of the heart the mouth speaks. The good person brings good things out of a good treasure, and the evil person brings evil things out of an evil treasure. I tell you, on the day of judgment you will have to give an account for every careless word you utter; for by your words you will be justified, and by your words you will be condemned."

To contemplate:

Jesus, God's own truthful servant,
    challenges his hearers
        to look again for truth.
They have seen him drive the demons out,
    yet accuse him of Satan's work,
        ruler of the world of lies.

"Comes good fruit from a tree that's bad,
  God's work from Satan's strength?
"The tree is known by its fruit.
  Your actions and your words reveal
    the desires of your heart."

Jesus, proclaimer of God's own truth,
  help me speak that precious truth
    and never tell the lie.

How can I hope to give account
  of my every thoughtless word,
    my careless words and acts?

A good tree or a bad am I?
  An indifferent tree, I fear,
    nor wholly good nor bad.

O saving Lord, you recognize
  no "in-between" or "neither nor"—
    with you, it's good or bad.

How can I then be saved, my Lord,
  unless you really stand for me
    my saving God-with-me?

The Sign of Jonah

Mt 12:38-42: *Then some of the scribes and Pharisees said to him, "Teacher, we wish to see a sign from you." But he answered them, "An evil and adulterous generation asks for a sign, but no sign will be given to it except the sign of the prophet Jonah. For just as Jonah was three days and three nights in the belly of the sea monster, so for three days and three nights the Son of Man will be in the heart of the earth. The people of Nineveh will rise up at the judgment with this generation and condemn it, because they repented at the proclamation of Jonah, and see, something greater than Jonah is here! The queen of the South will rise up at the judgment with this generation and condemn it, because she came from the ends of the earth to listen to the wisdom of Solomon, and see, something greater than Solomon is here!"*

To contemplate:

God sent Jonah upon a mission
    to save the people of Nineveh.
      But Jonah went the other way.
Why should he save his enemy?

As the story goes, there came a whale
    to swallow Jonah and spit him up—
    after three days and three dark nights—
upon a shore near Nineveh.

This story, Jesus says, is a sign
    of his own three days within the earth.
    His resurrection from the dead
will signify who he really is.
When Jonah preached to Nineveh,
    the people listened and repented.
    When Jesus preached in Galilee,
how many heard his words?

The queen of Sheba came to see
    the wonders wrought by Solomon;
    she tested his reputed wisdom
and found him equal to the trial.
Am I as eager to hear your word?
    Would I desire like this queen
    to listen to the deep wisdom
you speak within our midst?

O Jesus, greater prophet than Jonah was,
    and wiser far than Solomon,
    I see in you the hopes fulfilled
of all the prophets and all the wise!

The Returning Demon

Mt 12:43-45: *"When the unclean spirit has gone out of a person, it wanders through waterless regions looking for a resting place, but it finds none. Then it says, 'I will return to my house from which I came.' When it comes, it finds it empty, swept, and put in order. Then it goes and brings along seven other spirits more evil than itself, and they enter and live there; and the last state of that person is worse than the first. So will it be also with this evil generation."*

To contemplate:

Is not this the story of us all,
   even of those God chose
      to be his own,
   and lead the nations of the earth
      to find in him their one true God?

At first the people of Jesus' time
   come out to hear his words to them,
      admire his healing of their ills,
   then listen to his critics
      and fault his every act.

Is not this the story of my life—
    repeated turnings to my Lord,
        repeated fallings off from him?
    The spirit of evil I reject,
        yet secretly make place for him.
Does not it sometimes better seem
    never to have loved at all,
        than once to have loved and lost—
    better to have never followed Christ
        than to follow him, then quit?
O Lord, help me ever faithful be,
    no more to wander far from you
        in search of other love than yours.
    O Lord, I would remain with you!
        Remain, my loving God-with-me!

Mt 12:46-47 = Mk 3:31-32 Jesus' mother and brothers come to speak to him.

Who Are My Brothers and Sisters?

Mt 12:48-50: *"Who is my mother, and who are my brothers?" And pointing to his disciples, he said, "Here are my mother and my brothers! For whoever does the will of my Father in heaven is my brother and sister and mother."*

To contemplate:

One thing you want of us, dear Lord,
   one only thing—
to do our Father's holy will,
   his will for us.
One thing you want of me, my Lord,
   one only thing—
to do my Father's holy will,
   his will for me.
For if I do his holy will,
   you call me brother, sister;
and if I truly am your brother, your sister,
   God is my Father!
Then we who follow you, dear Lord,
   doing our Father's will,

all become your brothers, sisters—
    all, your family.
But how can we your mother be?
    Can we be Mary?
How can we be that holy maid
    who brought you life?
Only if we say with her:
    "Here am I,
the servant of the Lord;
    your will be done" (Lk 1:38).
If, like her, we seek God's will,
    we bring the world
his loving, only Son—
    we bring forth you!

O Jesus, my dear Emmanuel,
    I'll bring you forth
into a world that knows you not,
    our impoverished world.
But I am weak, my Lord, too weak
    to keep this promise—
unless you keep your promise first,
    to be my God-with-me.

Mt 13:1-15 = Mk 4:1-12 Parable of the sower.

Jesus Tells the Kingdom Truth

Mt 13:16-23: *"Blessed are your eyes, for they see, and your ears, for they hear. Truly I tell you, many prophets and righteous people longed to see what you see, but did not see it, and to hear what you hear, but did not hear it.*

"Hear then the parable of the sower. When anyone hears the word of the kingdom and does not understand it, the evil one comes and snatches away what is sown in the heart; this is what was sown on the path. As for what was sown on rocky ground, this is the one who hears the word and immediately receives it with joy; yet such a person has no root, but endures only for a while, and when trouble or persecution arises on account of the word, that person immediately falls away. As for what was sown among thorns, this is the one who hears the word, but the cares of the world and the lure of wealth choke the word, and it yields nothing. But as for what was sown on good soil, this is the one who hears the word and understands it, who indeed bears fruit and yields, in one case a hundredfold, in another sixty, and in another thirty."

To contemplate:

Ah Lord, I want to hear your word of kingdom truth.
  Sometimes I fail to hear, fail to see.
    You must help me, Lord!
  Jesus, you must be the faithful sower,
sower of truth about the kingdom of your Father.
Your truth, like seed, must sink into our hearts
  before it can grow and thrive in us;
    but our hearts are very hard,
  hard as the ground worn down by feet
careless of where they trod, indifferent to truth.

Sometimes our hearts are as hard as rocky ground
  where not a single root can enter in—
    "hearts of stone," we say.
  The superficial, rapid growth of stalk
will not endure the ridicule of lovers of the flesh.

And how often, Lord, your word encounters hearts
  already occupied with myriad thoughts
    and cares of this, our world.
  Like thorns, our worldly worries choke
your word and strangle the love you'd grow in us.

O Lord of the harvest, clear our poor, sick hearts
  of the harrying cares that overgrow
    our affection and our love.
  Open our ears and eyes and hearts
to your truth and love, O saving God-with-us.

At Harvest Time

Mt 13:24-30: *He put before them another parable: "The kingdom of heaven may be compared to someone who sowed good seed in his field; but while everybody was asleep, an enemy came and sowed weeds among the wheat, and then went away. So when the plants came up and bore grain, then the weeds appeared as well. And the slaves of the householder came and said to him, 'Master, did you not sow good seed in your field? Where, then, did these weeds come from?' He answered, 'An enemy has done this.' The slaves said to him, 'Then do you want us to go and gather them?' But he replied, 'No; for in gathering the weeds you would uproot the wheat along with them. Let both of them grow together until the harvest; and at harvest time I will tell the reapers, Collect the weeds first and bind them in bundles to be burned, but gather the wheat into my barn.'"*

To contemplate:

"The kingdom of heaven may be compared to
    someone
  who sowed good seed in his field."

That "someone" must be you, my Lord of the
   harvest—
   you yourself are the kingdom of God!
You sow yourself in the field of men and women,
   to grow in our minds and hearts;
you are the seed and we are your harvest field,
   for you are our God-within-us.

But we are confused and broken tracts of land,
   ill-suited for your wheat;
full of the weeds of lust and lies are we,
   the weeds of your mortal enemy.
Yet you bear with us, bear with all our faults
   until the time of harvest.
Then will you gather us in with all the good
   and all the evil we have done.

Then will there be a weighing out of good and bad,
   a final time of reckoning.
Those who identify themselves with bad will burn;
   those, with good, will glory.

O Lord of the harvest, Lord of the good and bad,
   have mercy on us.
O Lord of the world, judge of our good and bad,
   have mercy on me.
I place no trust in myself to pass your test;
   I am confused and weak.
I place my trust entirely in your hands,
   my saving God-with-me.

Mt 13:31-32 = Mk 4:30-32 Parable of the mustard seed.

Jesus Proclaims
What Has Been Hidden

Mt 13:33-35: *He told them another parable: "The kingdom of heaven is like yeast that a woman took and mixed in with three measures of flour until all of it was leavened."*

Jesus told the crowds all these things in parables; without a parable he told them nothing. This was to fulfill what had been spoken through the prophet:

"I will open my mouth to speak in parables;
I will proclaim what has been hidden
from the foundation of the world."

To contemplate:

At first, Matthew, you seem to suggest
   that Jesus speaks in parables
      to confuse his hearers (13:13-14).

But here you quote a prophetic psalm,
   showing he speaks his parables
      to reveal hidden truth—
hidden from the world's foundation,
   the beginning of our time—
      truth about our God.

Deep truth about his heavenly kingdom:
 like yeast that a woman mixed
  with a mass of flour,
Jesus, baker of God's bread,
 mixed love into the dead dough
  of our joyless world.

The yeast of his own life-giving love
 raises to life our lifeless lump—
  now bread fit for God!

O Lord of the bakery of the world,
 Lord Jesus Emmanuel,
  yeast of tasteless lives,
transform us into savory loaf,
 delight of our Father-God,
  to satisfy his taste!

He cannot but delight in us
 if you live in our hearts,
  our saving God-in-us.

The Kingdom of the Son of Man

Mt 13:36-43: *Then he left the crowds and went into the house. And his disciples approached him, saying, "Explain to us the parable of the weeds of the field." He answered, "The one who sows the good seed is the Son of Man; the field is the world, and the good seed are the children of the kingdom; the weeds are the children of the evil one, and the enemy who sowed them is the devil; the harvest is the end of the age, and the reapers are angels. Just as the weeds are collected and burned up with fire, so will it be at the end of the age. The Son of Man will send his angels, and they will collect out of his kingdom all causes of sin and all evildoers, and they will throw them into the furnace of fire, where there will be weeping and gnashing of teeth. Then the righteous will shine like the sun in the kingdom of their Father. Let anyone with ears listen!"*

To contemplate:

Into the field of this wide world
   strides the Son of Man
      to sow the good seed
         of his word of love.

Into this same field of our world
    snakes the evil one
        to sow the bad seed
            of his hateful lies.
And all of us must choose the seed
    that we will cultivate—
        good seed of the Son of Man
            or Satan's evil seed.
Then at the end of all our time
    the Son of Man will angels send
        to purify his kingdom,
            cast out the evil ones.

O Lord of the harvest of this world,
    I truly believe in you.
You are the Son of Man, my Lord,
    God's heir to all the world.
Your kingdom, Jesus, begins on earth;
    it will be fulfilled in heaven.
Both are really one great realm—
    the temporal here, eternal there.

You yourself, O Son of Man,
    will bring your harvest home,
to shine like the very sun itself
    in the kingdom of your Father.
        Harvest me, O Son of Man!

Hidden Treasure

Mt 13:44-46: *"The kingdom of heaven is like treasure hidden in a field, which someone found and hid; then in his joy he goes and sells all that he has and buys that field.*

"Again, the kingdom of heaven is like a merchant in search of fine pearls; on finding one pearl of great value, he went and sold all that he had and bought it."

To contemplate:

Is God's kingdom, Lord, such treasure
    that I must willingly
barter my possessions of this world
    for that eternal wealth?
What thing is worth the timeless prize?
    What home or car or any *thing*
can compensate for heaven's loss?
    Any skill or power, pleasure?
What relationship within this world
    is worth the loss of God?
Must not alliances that I form
    embrace me in his love?

Is God's kingdom, then, a shining pearl
     that I must bargain for
with all my gaudy earthly pearls—
     all for one eternal gem?

My saving Lord, I find it hard
     to grasp God's kingdom's worth.
My mind grips things I hear and see;
     my heart, people I touch.
Yet you are the kingdom merchant
     who searches for finest pearls.
You find them in your people, Lord;
     you gave your life for them!
Are we, then, pearls so valuable
     you gave your life for us?
Is that the price, the awful price
     you willingly paid for us?

Ah, Lord, I've found a dearest pearl,
     one pearl worth my whole life,
the shining pearl I call my bride—
     I'd give my life for her!
Together we cling to the ultimate pearl,
     the pearl worth all the rest,
     our Alpha and Omega!

The Good and the Bad

Mt 13:47-52: *"Again, the kingdom of heaven is like a net that was thrown into the sea and caught fish of every kind; when it was full, they drew it ashore, sat down, and put the good into baskets but threw out the bad. So it will be at the end of the age. The angels will come out and separate the evil from the righteous and throw them into the furnace of fire, where there will be weeping and gnashing of teeth.*

"Have you understood all this?" They answered, "Yes." And he said to them, "Therefore every scribe who has been trained for the kingdom of heaven is like the master of a household who brings out of his treasure what is new and what is old."

To contemplate:

A picture by the Sea of Galilee:
fishermen sort out the contents of their catch,
    separating bad fish from the good.
A second picture like this first:
angels are sorting out the kingdom people,
    separating bad persons from the good.

The kingdom with both good and bad
is the kingdom of the Son of Man on earth,
    this world of people good and bad.
    O Lord, when you send your angels out,
will they find me among good persons or the bad?
    Where will they find me, Lord?

Will they bear me up among the saved,
or let me sink in the fiery pit of regret
    for ignoring you, my saving Lord?
    Lord of the harvest, your sharp words
cut deep into my conscience, into my heart.
    I take your warning gravely, Lord.

And now a third picture you evoke:
a householder choosing from his store of goods
    objects that are new and old.
    Are you saying your kingdom, Lord,
includes truths of the Old Testament and New—
    the New builds upon the Old?

Lord of the house, you teach us true:
your kingdom comprises old truths and new.

    Unite us in your balance, Lord!

Mt 13:54-58 – Mk 6:1-6; Mt 14:1-21 = Mk 6:14-44 Jesus returns to
Nazareth; the Baptist's death.

Peter, the Sinking Rock

Mt 14:22-33: *He made the disciples get into the boat and go on ahead to the other side, while he dismissed the crowds. And after he had dismissed the crowds, he went up the mountain by himself to pray. When evening came, he was there alone, but by this time the boat, battered by the waves, was far from the land, for the wind was against them. And early in the morning he came walking toward them on the sea. But when the disciples saw him walking on the sea, they were terrified, saying, "It is a ghost!" And they cried out in fear. But immediately Jesus spoke to them and said, "Take heart, it is I; do not be afraid."*

Peter answered him, "Lord, if it is you, command me to come to you on the water." He said, "Come." So Peter...started walking on the water, and came toward Jesus. But when he noticed the strong wind, he became frightened, and beginning to sink, he cried out, "Lord, save me!" Jesus immediately reached out his hand and caught him, saying to him, "You of little faith, why did you doubt?" When they got into the boat, the wind ceased. And those in the boat worshiped him, saying, "Truly you are the Son of God."

To contemplate:

Fierce winds and waves of adversity
   assault the fragile boat, the Church,
      but Jesus, our saving God-with-us
      walks straight through wailing wind;
   over wild roaring waves he comes
to save his own from watery grave.

Brave Peter would walk on water, too,
   and when the Lord invites him "Come!"
      stout-heartedly he walks alone—
      but not for long! Strong wind
   frightens him, and down he sinks.
Jesus must reach out to bear him up.
Peter means "Rock," here "sinking rock,"
   not yet unwavering rock of faith
      upon whom to build the Church—
      he is still of little faith,
   must learn to look not at the waves
but only at his saving God-with-him.

O Lord of the raging sea, I, too,
   am one of little faith and trust.
      I call you the very Son of God,
      adore you as my saving Lord;
   yet half-heartedly I really fear
the raging wind and roaring sea.
      O Lord, reach your saving hand to me!

---

*Mt 14:34-15:11 = Mk 6:53-7:23 Jesus heals in Gennesaret; he rejects
the tradition of the elders against the fourth commandment.*

What Kind of Leader Will Peter Be?

Mt 15:12-16: *Then the disciples approached and said to him, "Do you know that the Pharisees took offense when they heard what you said [about substituting their own precepts for God's commandments]?" He answered, "Every plant that my heavenly Father has not planted will be uprooted. Let them alone; they are blind guides of the blind. And if one blind person guides another, both will fall into a pit." But Peter said to him, "Explain this parable to us." Then he said, "Are you also still without understanding?"*

To contemplate:

Peter still has much to learn,
    much more to understand
before he will be the foundation rock
    for Jesus' future Church.

Peter, would you become a beacon for us—
    a true guide?
Have you been planted by the Father,
    or simply by yourself?

By yourself you a blind
   leader of the blind.
But if the Father leads,
   you can guide us along his way.

O Lord, will you say the same of me,
   if I rely upon myself,
set up my mind as my only source
   of light to guide my acts?

Does not your parable tell us here
   conscience is our inner eye
to catch the light you shine on us,
   the light that is yourself?

O Peter, as our Lord has willed,
   reflect his light for me,
that I may see the way of faith
   into his kingdom's light.

Mt 15:21-16:12 = Mk 7:25-8:21 Jesus cures the Canaanite woman's daughter and many other people, feeds four thousand, rejects the demand for a sign, and scolds the disciples.

My Father Has Revealed
My Identity to You

Mt 16:13-18: *Now when Jesus came into the district of Caesarea Philippi, he asked his disciples, "Who do people say that the Son of Man is?" And they said, "Some say John the Baptist, but others Elijah, and still others Jeremiah or one of the prophets." He said to them, "But who do you say that I am?" Simon Peter answered, "You are the Messiah, the Son of the living God." And Jesus answered him, "Blessed are you, Simon son of Jonah! For flesh and blood has not revealed this to you, but my Father in heaven. And I tell you, you are Peter, and on this rock I will build my Church."*

To contemplate:

When the disciples saw their Lord
   come walking on the water

and calm the roaring wind and sea,
   they thought they grasped the truth:
"Truly, you are the Son of God!" (14:33).
   But later on when Jesus taught
"Beware the leaven of Pharisees,"
   they did not understand (16:6-12).

Then Jesus asked them who he was,
　　and only Peter answered:
"You are the Son of the living God!"

　　Yes, that was truly said,
for Peter spoke not human words
　　he learned from flesh and blood,
but words of far deeper truth,
　　revealed by God himself.
So now does Jesus name him "Rock"—
　　foundation of his Church;
at last his faith is not his own,
　　but gift of his Father-God.
Wild waves made him a sinking rock;
　　self-confidence blinded him.
But now he firmly stands, the Rock,
　　though he has more to learn.

O Father who in heaven dwells,
　　transform my little faith
into deep trust in Jesus Christ
　　as your only Son, divine.
O Jesus, bless me, too, as one who shares
　　Peter's belief in you.

On This Rock
I Will Build My Church

Mt 16:18-20: *"And I tell you, you are Peter, and on this rock I will build my church, and the gates of Hades will not prevail against it. I will give you the keys of the kingdom of heaven, and whatever you bind on earth will be bound in heaven, and whatever you loose on earth will be loosed in heaven." Then he sternly ordered the disciples not to tell anyone that he was the Messiah.*

To contemplate:

Now that the secret has been revealed,
   the secret of Jesus' identity,
      he reveals his own secret plan
   to found his Church on Peter, rock,
though he'd failed his trial upon the sea.
His faith, now firm in the Father's gift,
   becomes the strong foundation rock
      of the Church of Jesus Christ.
   Henceforth Peter unites the fold,
sheepfold of Jesus, Shepherd supreme.

Upon Peter as rock Jesus' Church will stand
    secure against all vile attacks
        of earth and even Satan's hell.
    As long as earth remains intact,
intact remains the Church of Christ.
To Peter, Jesus entrusts his keys
    that alone unlock the kingdom gates,
        keys of access to the Father,
    keys that bind and keys that loose
the portals of the Church on earth.
For the Church is God's kingdom, too,
    his temporal kingdom in the world
        waiting to be eternalized,
    when the final heavenly kingdom comes,
in the glory of Jesus and the Father.

Father, I'm awed by your gifts to us:
    your supreme gift of your own dear Son
        to poor, blinded sons and daughters;
    your gift of the Church as threshold firm
to your everlasting heavenly kingdom.
And Jesus, thanks for your gifts to us:
    your gift of authority in Peter—
        gift to us of this rock of faith,
    gift of security in our belief,
our key to eternal life with you.

Peter, the Stumbling Block

Mt 16:21-25: *From that time on, Jesus began to show his disciples that he must go to Jerusalem and undergo great suffering at the hands of the elders and chief priests and scribes, and be killed, and on the third day be raised. And Peter took him aside and began to rebuke him, saying, "God forbid it, Lord! This must never happen to you." But he turned and said to Peter, "Get behind me, Satan! You are a stumbling block to me; for you are setting your mind not on divine things but on human things."*

Then Jesus told his disciples, "If any want to become my followers, let them deny themselves and take up their cross and follow me. For those who want to save their life will lose it, and those who lose their life for my sake will find it."

To contemplate:

Jesus names Peter to be his rock,
   the rock of his true Church;
yet as soon as he foretells his plan
   of suffering in Jerusalem,

Peter would block him in his way
of doing his Father's will.
The man who just heard Jesus' word
of highest commendation,
now hears a far different word
of deepest condemnation.
Oh, awful shock of Jesus' word
to bumbling Peter: Satan!
"Behind me, Satan, stumbling block,
no longer rock of faith,
no longer rock of love for me,
but only stumbling rock.
Until you think the thoughts of God,
not just the thoughts of men,
you cannot be my rock of love,
but only Satan's stone."

Jesus, what harsh words are these.
And you add another word:
"To follow me, deny yourself,
take firmly up your cross!
To save your life, give it up to me;
then you can truly find it."
O Jesus, we can follow you,
take up our heavy cross,
only if you bear it, too—
our own Emmanuel!

Mt 16:26-17:23 = Mk 8:34-9:32 The transfiguration and cure of the demoniac boy.

Peter Speaks and Acts for Jesus

Mt 17:24-27: *When they reached Capernaum, the collectors of the temple tax came to Peter and said, "Does your teacher not pay the temple tax?" He said, "Yes, he does." And when he came home, Jesus spoke of it first, asking, "What do you think, Simon? From whom do kings of the earth take toll or tribute? From their children or from others?" When Peter said, "From others," Jesus said to him, "Then the children are free. However, so that we do not give offense to them, go to the sea and cast a hook; take the first fish that comes up; and when you open its mouth, you will find a coin; take that and give it to them for you and me."*

To contemplate:

This curious little fish story
    illustrates a point:
Peter already speaks for Jesus,
    and acts in his behalf.
Even the temple tax collectors
    recognize in Peter
authority to speak for Jesus
    and answer for his cause.

Peter has been learning the lesson,
  hard lesson of "stumbling block,"
for now Jesus enlightens him
  on how to think like God.

The Father spares his own dear sons
  the law of the temple tax.
Yet the teacher wishes no offense,
  sends Peter to pay the tax.

Peter, professional fisherman,
  must use his skill to pay;
with a little help of his guiding Lord,
  he finds the coin he needs.

O Jesus, my sensitive teacher,
  with Peter I would learn
our Father's will for our daily lives
  as God's good citizens.

Teach us, Lord, to do our part
  as leaven for our world;
be here with us to see us through,
  though it take a miracle!

Mt 18:1-9 = Mk 9:33-50 Jesus teaches child-like humility, and warns against scandal.

Jesus Is Our Good Shepherd

Mt 18:10-14: *"Take care that you do not despise one of these little ones; for, I tell you, in heaven their angels continually see the face of my Father.... What do you think? If a shepherd has a hundred sheep, and one of them has gone astray, does he not leave the ninety-nine on the mountains and go in search of the one that went astray? And if he finds it, truly I tell you, he rejoices over it more than over the ninety-nine that never went astray. So it is not the will of your Father in heaven that one of these little ones should be lost."*

To contemplate:

Astounding value God sees in us,
   in his infinite loving care!
He sends his angels who see his face
   to protect us on our way.

More astounding still, he sends to us
   his own Son as our shepherd!
If one of a hundred sheep is lost,
   our Good Shepherd seeks it out.

Up rocky precipice climbs he,
   down perilous canyon steep;
Jesus himself comes after us
   to claim us for his own.

Why do we worry, then, so much?
   What have we to fear?

Nothing, if we really are his,
   submit ourselves to him
as little ones who seek his love
   and try to follow him.

O Jesus, be my shepherd, too,
   count me among your flock;

bring me to your Father's house
   to see him face to face,

with the holy angel he's given me,
   see him face to face.

Lord Jesus, I rejoice with you,
   my saving God-with-me!

Whatever You Bind on Earth

Mt 18:15-20: *"If another member of the Church sins against you, go and point out the fault when the two of you are alone. If the member listens to you, you have regained that one. But if you are not listened to, take one or two others along with you, so that every word may be confirmed by the evidence of two or three witnesses. If the member refuses to listen to them, tell it to the Church; and if the offender refuses to listen even to the Church, let such a one be to you as a Gentile and a tax collector. Truly I tell you, whatever you bind on earth will be bound in heaven, and whatever you loose on earth will be loosed in heaven. Again, truly I tell you, if two of you agree on earth about anything you ask, it will be done for you by my Father in heaven. For where two or three are gathered in my name, I am there among them."*

To contemplate:

A process of reconciliation
   and brotherly-sisterly correction:
      simple conversation first,
         then calm confrontation;

finally involve the Church itself
in judgment of the argument
with verdict to bind or loose.
Unlike other associations,
the Church can make decisions
with eternal repercussions.
What it binds or looses here
is bound or loosed in heaven!
Members of the Church can count
on God's own ratification.
And when we pray in unison
to ask divine assistance,
we know our heavenly Father
will listen to our cause.
For where two of us or three
gather in Jesus' name,
he is even here with us.

O Jesus, our God-with-us,
we pray for lasting union,
that we may love each other
in catholic harmony.
In your love, our kingdom Lord,
we live with one another,
and pray for all our needs.

Then Father-sent Emmanuel,
live and pray with us!

I Am There among You

Mt 18:19-20: *"Again, truly I tell you, if two of you agree on earth about anything you ask, it will be done for you by my Father in heaven. For where two or three are gathered in my name, I am there among them."*

To contemplate:

Father, we believe your Son,
    and gather in his Church
to pray together for our needs,
    in love for one another.
We know you hear our prayer, dear God,
    for your Jesus prays with us.
He's there within our very midst,
    just as he said he'd be.

Lord Jesus, two of us on earth
    agreed on one great thing—
that we belong to one another
    everlastingly!
Most solemnly we said, "I do"—
    said it as a prayer;

by far the most impassioned prayer
  that we have ever said.
We said "I do" to one another
  in church before your priest;
and all our friends did witness it,
  as we together wed.
We were together in your name,
  dear Lord, united there
with you as our chief witness
  and provider of our feast (Jn 2).
And so we call upon you now,
  confiding in your word
that you remain here with us, Lord,
  presiding in our home.
And everything we do together,
  we do with you, dear Lord.
You are the love that makes us one,
  the love sustaining ours.
You are the bond between us, Lord,
  the same covenant bond
that unites your Church with God (Eph 5:32).
Jesus, be our bond of love!

Forgive As the Father
Has Forgiven You

Mt 18:21-35: *Then Peter came and said to him, "Lord, if another...sins against me, how often should I forgive? As many as seven times?" Jesus said to him, "Not seven times, but, I tell you, seventy-seven times.*

"For this reason the kingdom of heaven may be compared to a king who wished to settle accounts with his slaves.... One who owed him ten thousand talents was brought to him.... The slave fell on his knees before him, saying, 'Have patience with me, and I will pay you everything.' And out of pity for him, the lord of that slave released him and forgave him the debt. But that same slave, as he went out, came upon one of his fellow slaves who owed him a hundred denarii; and seizing him by the throat, he said, 'Pay what you owe.' Then his fellow slave fell down and pleaded with him, 'Have patience with me, and I will pay you.' But he refused.... His lord summoned him and said to him, 'You wicked slave! I forgave you all that debt because you pleaded with me. Should you not have had mercy on your fellow slave, as I had mercy on you?' And in anger his lord handed him over to be tortured until he would pay his entire debt. So my heavenly Father will also do to every one of you, if you do not forgive your brother or sister from your heart."

To contemplate:

Ah, Peter, there you go again,
  presuming to know all answers.
Seven times sounds like a good round number,
      but not to Jesus—
  he demands much more, seventy seven!
  Lord, how could I ever forgive
  so many times as you demand?
But when I look at all my own offenses
      against our Father,
  seventy-seven times is but the start!
  Jesus, your story of the servant
  who received his Lord's forgiveness,
yet refused forgiveness to his fellow servant,
      cuts close to home.
  Is that the way I treat the others?

  O Father, you are the Lord of all,
  the Lord who loves us every one
as sons and daughters in your great kingdom.
      Have mercy, Lord,
  for we are guilty of offenses multiple.
  In this quiet moment of my heart
  I do forgive my brothers, sisters
who've injured me in any way or hurt my pride.
      Forgive me also, Lord.

Mt 19:1-9 = Mk 10:1-12 Jesus rejects divorce.

Celibacy for the Kingdom of Heaven

Mt 19:9-12: *"I say to you, whoever divorces his wife (unless the marriage is unlawful) and marries another commits adultery." [His] disciples said to him, "If that is the case of a man with his wife, it is better not to marry." He answered, "Not all can accept [this] word, but only those to whom it is granted. Some are incapable of marriage because they were born so; some, because they were made so by others; some, because they have renounced marriage for the sake of the kingdom of heaven. Whoever can accept this ought to accept it"* (Revised NAB).

To contemplate:

When Jesus admits of no divorce
   from lawfully married spouse,
his disciples protest that he demands
   too much sacrifice:
"Better not to marry!" they cry.
   He partially agrees:
"Those who give up wedded life
   do the harder thing—

but only those who give it up
   for a great ideal,
as sign of God's heavenly kingdom
   to those who live in marriage.
In heaven there is no marrying (22:30),
   no need of bodily love:
in God they supremely love each other;
   no need of procreation
to prolong their life in progeny—
   their own life is eternal.
Thus those who marry give a sign
   to those who marry not,
a sign of intense, dynamic love
   of spouses for each other,
a sign of the love that's possible
   in God's earthly kingdom.
And those who forego married love
   also give a sign,
a sign of the universal love
   in God's heavenly kingdom."
Thus Jesus blesses both the love
   of those who live in marriage
and the virginal love of celibates
   who give their lives to God.
Lord, help us mutually give these signs
   of your Emmanuel-love.

Mt 19:13-30 = Mk 10:13-31 Jesus blesses children and warns against riches.

The Father's Generosity

Mt 20:1-16: *"For the kingdom of heaven is like a landowner who went out early in the morning to hire laborers for his vineyard. After agreeing with the laborers for the usual daily wage, he sent them into his vineyard.... When he went out again about noon and about three o'clock, he did the same. And about five o'clock he went out and found others standing around.... He said to them, 'You also go into the vineyard.' When evening came, the owner of the vineyard said to his manager, 'Call the laborers and give them their pay, beginning with the last and then going to the first.' When those hired about five o'clock came, each of them received the usual daily wage. Now when the first came, they thought they would receive more; but each of them also received the usual daily wage. And when they received it, they grumbled against the landowner, saying, 'These last worked only one hour, and you have made them equal to us who have borne the burden of the day and the scorching heat.' But he replied to one of them, 'Friend, I am doing you no wrong; did you not agree with me for the usual daily wage? Take what belongs to you and go; I choose to give to this last the same as I give to you. Am I not allowed to do what I choose with what belongs to*

me? Or are you envious because I am generous?' So the
last will be first, and the first will be last."

To contemplate:

Dear Lord, what are we to make of such a tale—
    an employer so capricious as you paint him here?
How can he image the God of justice absolute,
    yet treat the first as last, the last as first?

Why offend our sense of justice with a story
    that spoils the portrait you have drawn of God,
your portrait of a kind and loving Father-God
    of even-handed justice for all his children?

Are you saying, "God's way is not confined to ours;
    we cannot therefore call him to account;
for he is, indeed, the God of boundless freedom,
    who can combine his justice with his mercy"?

Deep down you tell us he gave us all we have—
    that the one who has all he needs for life
cannot complain God did not give him more,
    for he did nothing to deserve the less.

And the wage God gives for our lifetime work—
    long or short in the vineyard of his world—
is the gift of eternal life, purest gift of all,
    same gift for all his children, great or small.
O Jesus, Lord of the vineyard, we give you thanks!

He Will Be Crucified!

Mt 20:17-19: *While Jesus was going up to Jerusalem, he took the twelve disciples aside by themselves, and said to them on the way, "See, we are going up to Jerusalem, and the Son of man will be handed over to the chief priests and scribes, and they will condemn him to death; then they will hand him over to the Gentiles to be mocked and flogged and crucified; and on the third day he will be raised."*

To contemplate:

Mark reported Jesus' prophecy
   he would be condemned
and handed over to the Gentiles
   to be mocked and scourged and killed.

But *"crucified"* is Matthew's word.
   Did Jesus really know
his future in such bloody detail—
   foresee his crucifixion?

Matthew, did you have access
   to apostolic tradition
other evangelists did not know?
   Or did you here insert
as prophecy on Jesus' lips,
   knowledge after the fact?

A question without clear answer!
   What is the real difference
between facing unknown horrible death
   and death by crucifixion?

My Jesus, whether you knew details
   or read the gathering gloom,
you held fast to your Father's mission
   till its logical conclusion.

You knew your steady revelation
   of our great Father-God
would so displease some priests and scribes
   they'd plot your bitter end.

O Jesus, marching on toward death,
   I, too, must face life's end.
Be with me through the gathering gloom
   to find our Father there!

---

*Mt 20:20-21:22 = Mk 10:35-11:25 Jesus rejects ambition, heals two
blind men, enters Jerusalem, cleanses the temple, and curses the bar-
ren fig tree.*

The Two Sons

Mt 21:23-32: *When he entered the temple, the chief priests and the elders of the people came to him as he was teaching, and said, "...Who gave you this authority?" Jesus said to them, "I will also ask you one question.... Did the baptism of John come from heaven, or was it of human origin?"... They answered Jesus, "We do not know." And he said to them, "Neither will I tell you by what authority I am doing these things.*

"What do you think? A man had two sons; he went to the first and said, 'Son, go and work in the vineyard today.' He answered, 'I will not'; but later he changed his mind and went. The father went to the second and said the same; and he answered, 'I go, sir'; but he did not go. Which of the two did the will of his father?" They said, "The first." Jesus said to them, "Truly I tell you, the tax collectors and the prostitutes are going into the kingdom of God ahead of you. For John came to you in the way of righteousness and you did not believe him, but the tax collectors and the prostitutes believed him; and even after you saw it, you did not change your minds and believe him."

To contemplate:

Another image of God's vineyard—
    this time to teach obedience.
Our Father calls us all to work
    for a better harvest crop.

Some who thought themselves holy
    pretended to answer "Yes" to God,
        but they did not do his will.

The tax collectors and prostitutes
    seemed to answer "No" to God;
yet they tried to obey his will,
    revealed to them by John.

Now a greater than John speaks to us:
    the only Son the Father sent,
        our true Emmanuel.

My Lord, we do not judge as you;
    we judge by outward sign,
We condemn a person for saying "No"—
    we cannot see the heart.
Am I like the son who says "No" but goes,
    or the son who says "Yes" but stays?
Is my obedience real or feigned?
    Is my heart true to you?

Mt 21:33-46 = Mk 12:1-12 Parable of the wicked tenants.

The Great Wedding Feast

Mt 22:2-14: *"The kingdom of heaven may be compared to a king who gave a wedding banquet for his son. He sent his slaves to call those who had been invited to the wedding banquet, but they would not come. Again he sent other slaves, saying, 'Tell those who have been invited: Look, I have prepared my dinner...and everything is ready; come to the wedding banquet.' But they made light of it and went away, one to his farm, another to his business, while the rest seized his slaves, mistreated them, and killed them. The king was enraged. He sent his troops, destroyed those murderers, and burned their city. Then he said to his slaves, 'The wedding is ready, but those invited were not worthy. Go therefore into the main streets, and invite everyone you find to the wedding banquet.' Those slaves went out into the streets and gathered all whom they found, both good and bad; so the wedding hall was filled with guests.*

"But when the king came in to see the guests, he noticed a man there who was not wearing a wedding robe, and he said to him, 'Friend, how did you get in here without a wedding robe?' And he was speechless. Then the king said to the attendants, 'Bind him hand and foot, and throw him into the outer darkness, where there will

be weeping and gnashing of teeth.' For many are called, but few are chosen."

To contemplate:

God invites us to heaven's wedding feast.
But are we too occupied with earthly goods
to bother with heaven's feast?

O Jesus, do you not warn us here
of our forgetfulness of God
in search of earthly goods?

And if we do accept God's summons,
yet fail to clothe ourselves
with his wedding robe of love,
the king, our God, won't welcome us
into the everlasting joy
of his almighty presence.

O Jesus, cover us with your wedding robe (Gal 3:27)
that we may enjoy God's feast
enfolded in your love!

Mt 22:15-33 = Mk 12:13-27 Jesus answers questions about taxes and the resurrection.

The Two Great Commandments

Mt 22:34-40: *When the Pharisees heard that he had si-lenced the Sadducees, they gathered together, and one of them, a lawyer, asked him a question to test him. "Teacher, which commandment in the law is the great-est?" He said to him, "'You shall love the Lord your God with all your heart, and with all your soul, and with all your mind.' This is the greatest and first commandment. And a second is like it: 'You shall love your neighbor as yourself.' On these two commandments hang all the law and the prophets."*

To contemplate:

Jesus combines all laws in love—
   "Love God above all else;
and love your neighbor as yourself.
   Love God with all your heart;
   love him with all your soul;
   love him with all your mind.
Then love your neighbor as his child."

O Lord of love, enrich our hearts,
    with the treasure of your love.
Nothing have I that is not yours;
    if, then, I can love at all,
it must be with your love for me.

O, you who have loved me first,
    project your love through me,
into the very heart of God,
    into all human hearts.

Above all, let me return your love;
    for in loving you as Lord,
I love all men and women, too,
    all those you came to save.

And in loving you, my own dear Lord,
    I love my God-with-me.

Mt 22:41-46 = Mk 13:35-37 Jesus proposes a question about David's son.

Jesus Condemns Hypocrisy

Mt 23:2-22: *"The scribes and the Pharisees sit on Moses' seat; therefore, do whatever they teach you and follow it; but do not do as they do, for they do not practice what they teach. They tie up heavy burdens, hard to bear, and lay them on the shoulders of others; but they themselves are unwilling to lift a finger to move them. They do all their deeds to be seen by others.... The greatest among you will be your servant. All who exalt themselves will be humbled, and all who humble themselves will be exalted.*

"But woe to you, scribes and Pharisees, hypocrites! For you lock people out of the kingdom of heaven. For you do not go in yourselves, and when others are going in, you stop them....

"Woe to you, blind guides, who say.... 'Whoever swears by the altar is bound by nothing, but whoever swears by the gift that is on the altar is bound by the oath.' How blind you are! For which is greater, the gift or the altar that makes the gift sacred? So whoever swears by the altar, swears by it and by everything on it; and whoever swears by the sanctuary, swears by it and by the one who dwells in it; and whoever swears by

heaven, swears by the throne of God and by the one who is seated upon it."

To contemplate:

My Lord, your strong words of warning
   challenge me to look into my life
      to weed out all hypocrisies,
         both great and small.
Do I blame my failings upon those of others—
   miss Mass because "the sermon's bad,"
      give little to the Church and say,
         "It helps me not"?

Do I expect more of others than myself—
   fail to do what I prescribe for them,
      lay heavy blame upon the young,
         yet help them not?
Which deeds do I perform to be seen by all,
   pretending modesty in my work,
      hoping for others' praise
         as model Christian?

Do I use striking words to "prove my point,"
   or depend upon the truth I speak?
      Do I swear and vow and testify,
         or simply bare my heart?

Dear Lord, unlock the motives from which I hide,
   root out all my hypocrisy.

Justice, Mercy, Faith

Mt 23:23-35: *"Woe to you, scribes and Pharisees, hypocrites! For you...have neglected the weightier matters of the law: justice and mercy and faith. It is these you ought to have practiced without neglecting the others. You blind guides! You strain out a gnat but swallow a camel!*

"Woe to you, scribes and Pharisees, hypocrites! For you clean the outside of the cup and of the plate, but inside they are full of greed and self-indulgence....

"Woe to you, scribes and Pharisees, hypocrites! For you are like whitewashed tombs, which on the outside look beautiful, but inside they are full of the bones of the dead....

"Woe to you, scribes and Pharisees, hypocrites! For you build the tombs of the prophets.... [but you are really] descendants of those who murdered the prophets. Fill up, then, the measure of your ancestors. You snakes, you brood of vipers! How can you escape being sentenced to hell? Therefore I send you prophets, sages, and scribes, some of whom you will kill and crucify, and some you will flog in your synagogues and pursue from town to town, so that upon you may come all the righteous blood shed on earth...."

To contemplate:

"Justice and mercy and faith"—
    these are your demands.

Justice that judges with equity,
    ignoring not great for small,
        not camels for gnats.
Justice that cuts through all facade
    of clean outside to see within
        the darkness there.
Justice instead of false legality,
    justice that hides no filth
        in whitewashed tomb.

Mercy for the offender who repents;
    though the offense be great,
        let mercy be greater still.

Have faith in what the prophets said,
    who spoke the words of God
        to call forth your belief.

Have faith in the apostles I will send
    to save you from your plight
        and preach my truth.

O Jesus, give me your justice, mercy,
    and your great gift of faith.

As a Hen Gathers Her Brood

Mt 23:37-39: *"Jerusalem, Jerusalem, the city that kills the prophets and stones those who are sent to it! How often have I desired to gather your children together as a hen gathers her brood under her wings, and you were not willing! See, your house is left to you, desolate. For I tell you, you will not see me again until you say, 'Blessed is the one who comes in the name of the Lord.'"*

To contemplate:

Thanks, Matthew, for this glimpse
   into the heart of Christ—
Messiah who laments Jerusalem,
   the city that Jesus loves,
   the city where he will die!
Thanks for a beautiful image of Jesus
   gathering chicks, as does a hen,
   under protecting wings.

He grieves over his lost people,
   unwilling to return his love,
   source of true happiness.

He grieves for their lost temple,
  to be made desolate, destroyed
  by the mighty Roman army.

He grieves most over their rejection
  of the word he's brought from God,
  word of heaven's kingdom.
He grieves that when he comes again,
  he will not find them ready
  for his final judgment.

O Jesus, Lord of final judgment,
  will you find me ready,
  ready for your kingdom?
Will you stoop to gather me,
  a wandering, stumbling chick,
  under protecting wing?

How I long for your loving arm
  to hold me close to you,
  my saving God-with-me.
How I yearn for your loving word
  inviting me home to you,
  home, into your kingdom!

Whoever Endures to the End
Will Be Saved

Mt 24:1-14: *As Jesus came out of the temple and was going away, his disciples came to point out to him the buildings of the temple. Then he asked them, "You see all these, do you not? Truly I tell you, not one stone will be left here upon another; all will be thrown down."*

...The disciples came to him privately, saying, "Tell us, when will this be, and what will be the sign of your coming and of the end of the age?" Jesus answered them, "Beware that no one leads you astray. For many will come in my name, saying, 'I am the Messiah!' and they will lead many astray....

"Then they will hand you over to be tortured and will put you to death, and you will be hated by all nations because of my name. Then many will fall away, and they will betray one another and hate one another. And many false prophets will arise and lead many astray. And because of the increase of lawlessness, the love of many will grow cold. But the one who endures to the end will be saved. And this good news of the kingdom will be proclaimed throughout the world, as a testimony to all the nations; and then the end will come."

To contemplate:

"Not one stone will be left here upon another."
  What a scene of utter desolation!
Nothing left to show that once was here
  God's place of dwelling with his people.
Yet the disciples have more than the temple here:
  they come to Jesus for the answers.
They ask the questions few today dare ask,
  questions that reach beyond the grave.

He warns them not to be led astray from him,
  not to follow after false Messiahs,
nor fear the torturers they will have to face
  for remaining true to him.

Worst of all, "the love of many will grow cold."
  What tragedy—love itself grows cold!
We cannot guarantee our love, cannot reassure
  ourselves our love will never fail.

Yet fragile creatures that we are, we have the hope
  that Christ himself now lives in us,
builds up our love, enduring to the end,
  till his good-news kingdom comes.

Dear Lord, we place our final trust in you,
  confident your love will never fail;
we look forward to your second coming,
  for you yourself are saving judge!

Mt 24:15-37 = Mk 13:14-32 Jesus teaches about the end of the world.

Keep Awake!

Mt 24:38-51: *"As in those days before the flood they were eating and drinking, marrying and giving in marriage, until the day Noah entered the ark, and they knew nothing until the flood came and swept them all away, so too will be the coming of the Son of Man. Then two will be in the field; one will be taken and one will be left.... Keep awake therefore, for you do not know on what day your Lord is coming. But understand this: if the owner of the house had known in what part of the night the thief was coming, he would have stayed awake and would not have let his house be broken into. Therefore you also must be ready, for the Son of Man is coming at an unexpected hour.*

"Who then is the faithful and wise slave, whom his master has put in charge of his household, to give the other slaves their allowance of food at the proper time? Blessed is that slave whom his master will find at work when he arrives. Truly I tell you, he will put that one in charge of all his possessions. But if that wicked slave says to himself, 'My master is delayed,' and he begins to beat his fellow slaves, and eats and drinks with drunkards, the master of that slave will come on a day when he does not expect him and at an hour that he does not

know. He will cut him in pieces and put him with the
hypocrites, where there will be weeping and gnashing of
teeth."

To contemplate:

O Son of Man, you will come for me!
  I believe your warning to keep awake,
not be caught unknowing, unprepared,
  rather to expect the secret hour.
O Son of Man, my hour is coming;
  the hour of my death, the last of life—
nears with each year, each day, each hour,
  until at last I yield up my life.

Will you be there? Undoubtedly!
  But will it be as Son of Man, our judge?
Or will you come as first you came to us—
  compassionate Jesus, saving God-with-us?

  It will be as both,
for the Son of Man is my saving judge.

Like a thief you'll come when I least expect,
  but not to rob my life nor cast me out.

O Son of Man, come at last, at last for me;
  save me from the place of grinding teeth...

  and bring me to our eternal home!

Wise and Foolish Virgins

Mt 25:1-13: *"Then the kingdom of heaven will be like this. Ten bridesmaids took their lamps and went to meet the bridegroom. Five of them were foolish, and five were wise. When the foolish took their lamps, they took no oil with them; but the wise took flasks of oil with their lamps. As the bridegroom was delayed, all of them became drowsy and slept. But at midnight there was a shout, 'Look! Here is the bridegroom! Come out to meet him.' Then all those bridesmaids got up and trimmed their lamps. The foolish said to the wise, 'Give us some of your oil, for our lamps are going out.' But the wise replied, 'No! there will not be enough for you and for us; you had better go to the dealers and buy some for yourselves.' And while they went to buy it, the bridegroom came, and those who were ready went with him into the wedding banquet; and the door was shut. Later the other bridesmaids came also, saying, 'Lord, lord, open to us.' But he replied, 'Truly I tell you, I do not know you.' Keep awake therefore, for you know neither the day nor the hour."*

To contemplate:

The foolish people look only at the present;
   the wise look forward to the future.
The foolish fail to envision what they'll need;
   the wise prepare to meet the groom.

And when he comes, the foolish are surprised;
   the wise are ready and prepared.
O Jesus, lordly bridegroom of our race,
   we hunger for your coming feast.

Which group is mine, the foolish or the wise?
   Am I waiting for you, well equipped
with stock of good works in my traveling bag,
   ready at any moment for your knock?

Lord of the wedding, I believe you'll come;
   yet I know I cannot be prepared,
unless you grant the oil for my lamp;
   of myself I am foolish and weak.

For my good works, I depend on you;
   without your grace I can nothing do.
The light of my lamp is but borrowed light,
   reflecting you, Light of the world.

Supply my flickering lamp with oil
   that I may see the way to you.
Then will I be well prepared
   to see your face at *our wedding feast!*

Wise and Foolish Servants

Mt 25:14-30: *"It [the coming of the kingdom] is as if a man, going on a journey, summoned his slaves and entrusted his property to them; to one he gave five talents, to another two, to another one, to each according to his ability.... The one who had received the five talents went off at once and traded with them, and made five more talents.... But the one who had received the one talent went off and...hid his master's money. After a long time the master of those slaves came and settled accounts with them. Then the one who had received the five talents came forward, bringing five more talents, saying, 'Master, you handed over to me five talents; see, I have made five more talents.' His master said to him, 'Well done, good and trustworthy slave; you have been trustworthy in a few things, I will put you in charge of many things; enter into the joy of your master....' Then the one who had received the one talent also came forward, saying, 'Master...I was afraid, and I went and hid your talent in the ground. Here you have what is yours.' But his master replied, 'You wicked and lazy slave!... Take the talent from him, and give it to the one with the ten talents. For to all those who have, more will be given, and they will have an abundance; but from those who have*

nothing, even what they have will be taken away. As for this worthless slave, throw him into the outer darkness, where there will be weeping and gnashing of teeth.'"

To contemplate:

Lord God, I believe the teacher you have sent,
   your own dear Son who here reveals
     your gifts to all of us.

Your gifts help us take a decisive part
   to make your kingdom come
     here upon our earth.

To use these gifts to make your kingdom grow—
   that is what you will for us—
     so your Son reveals.

O Lord, our King, I dread the fate of him
   who failed to use his single talent
     for your enterprise.

I long to share the prize of prudent ones
   who used their talents well for you,
     and thus shared your joy.

Father, thank you for all your gifts to me.
   I gratefully resolve to use them all
     to make your kingdom grow.
   Jesus, my Teacher and my King,
     share your joy with me!

"You Did It for Me!"

Mt 25:31-40: *"When the Son of Man comes in his glory, and all the angels with him, then he will sit on the throne of his glory. All the nations will be gathered before him, and he will separate people one from another as a shepherd separates the sheep from the goats, and he will put the sheep at his right hand and the goats at the left. Then the king will say to those at his right hand, 'Come, you that are blessed by my Father, inherit the kingdom prepared for you from the foundation of the world; for I was hungry and you gave me food, I was thirsty and you gave me something to drink, I was a stranger and you welcomed me, I was naked and you gave me clothing, I was sick and you took care of me, I was in prison and you visited me.' Then the righteous will answer him, 'Lord, when was it that we saw you hungry and gave you food, or thirsty and gave you something to drink? And when was it that we saw you a stranger and welcomed you, or naked and gave you clothing? And when was it that we saw you sick or in prison and visited you?' And the king will answer them, 'Truly I tell you, just as you did it to one of the least of these who are members of my family, you did it to me.'"*

To contemplate:

Marvelous image of marvelous king!
The judge of all the nations is the Son of Man,
   the God of angels who became a man
to experience all our human joys and sorrows,
   the limitations and emotions
      that motivate our acts.
The judge of all the nations is our God-with-us,
      who also is a man-with-us,
   and therefore judges all our acts,
      our very life itself,
from within perspectives that he shares with us,
   feelings and acts he finds in us.

The love that brought him down to us
   is the love that he expects of us,
   and the love with which he judges us.
The love with which we treat our brothers, sisters,
   is the love we give our God-with-us.
      He identifies with us!
How, then, can we fail life's greatest test?
      Only if we fail to love
      our fellow men and women.
   The people with whom we live and work
      are the people we must love—
the people with whom our judge identifies himself.

Marvelous image of marvelous king—
   the judge of nations is our God-with-us!

"You Didn't Do It for Me!"

Mt 25:41-46: *"Then he will say to those at his left hand, 'You that are accursed, depart from me into the eternal fire prepared for the devil and his angels; for I was hungry and you gave me no food, I was thirsty and you gave me nothing to drink, I was a stranger and you did not welcome me, naked and you did not give me clothing, sick and in prison and you did not visit me.' Then they also will answer, 'Lord, when was it that we saw you hungry or thirsty or a stranger or naked or sick or in prison, and did not take care of you?' Then he will answer them, 'Truly I tell you, just as you did not do it to one of the least of these, you did not do it to me.' And these will go away into eternal punishment, but the righteous into eternal life."*

To contemplate:

O King of all the world,
we know your judgment's right.
Not only have you created us
and known us head to foot;
you have become one of us,
felt our feelings,

thought our thoughts,
and lived our human life.
You have rejoiced with the rejoicing,
agonized with the agonizing.
You have known hunger, thirst and homelessness.
You've dealt with sickness and despair.
You have felt rejection,
torture, ridicule—
crucifixion!
You've felt all these things in your own flesh
and in the souls of men and women
in whom you've dwelt,
Emmanuel.

So we're not surprised, O Lord of all the world,
at the vehemence of your judgment
of those who reject their brothers, sisters,
or ignore them in their needs.

This, then, I ask of you, my judge-in-me:
the next time that I see a starving man or woman,
a homeless or half-naked man,
a grieving or despairing woman,
move me to reach out with loving care,
not pass on down the street.
Too often have I qualified for hell
by ignoring another's hell!

The
Passion
and
Resurrection

To Be Crucified!

Mt 26:1-5: *When Jesus had finished saying all these things, he said to his disciples, "You know that after two days the Passover is coming, and the Son of Man will be handed over to be crucified."*

Then the chief priests and the elders of the people gathered in the palace of the high priest, who was called Caiaphas, and they conspired to arrest Jesus by stealth and kill him. But they said, "Not during the festival, or there may be a riot among the people."

To contemplate:

O Jesus, you know what you are facing now,
   you know you have but two days more
      to escape cruel crucifixion.
Yet you hold the course your Father wills,
   the commission he has given you
      to save us by your death.

Great mystery of the Father's love for us!
   Mystery of your love for him,
      and of your love for us!

And did you also know who'd hand you over,
    hand you to the Roman soldiers
        to be cruelly crucified?

Yes, you felt the intense hostility
    of chief priests and elders,
        the vacillation of the mob—
            the treachery of a friend!

Yet even while we were most grievous sinners
    you sacrificed your life for us—
        even for us sinners (Rom 5:8).
How can I ever repay your merciful love,
    make up for even half my sins—
        how thank you by my life?

———————

Mt 26:6-19 = Mk 14:3-16 A woman anoints Jesus; Judas betrays him. The disciples prepare for the Passover meal.

This Is My Body, My Blood

Mt 26:20-30: *When it was evening [of the first day of the Feast of Unleavened Bread], he took his place with the twelve; and while they were eating, he said, "Truly I tell you, one of you will betray me...." Judas, who betrayed him, said, "Surely not I, Rabbi?" He replied, "You have said so."*

While they were eating, Jesus took a loaf of bread, and after blessing it he broke it, gave it to the disciples, and said, "Take, eat; this is my body." Then he took a cup, and after giving thanks he gave it to them, saying, "Drink from it, all of you; for this is my blood of the covenant, which is poured out for many for the forgiveness of sins. I tell you, I will never again drink of this fruit of the vine until that day when I drink it new with you in my Father's kingdom." When they had sung the hymn, they went out to the Mount of Olives.

To contemplate:

He knows the man who will betray him
    this last night of his life.
Yet calmly he sits there with his men,
    feasting as if all were well.

This Passover meal he takes with them
    is his last meal before his death.
This bread he changes into his body
    is the last food he will impart.
This wine he changes into his blood
    is the last drink he will give.

The blood of Moses' covenant
    was the lifeblood of young bulls (Ex 24:6).
The blood of Jesus' covenant
    is his lifeblood shed for us—
shed the day after this Eucharist,
    shed on bleak Calvary!

How can Jesus give up so much?
    How can he love so much?
His Father entrusts to him a work:
    to save us from our sins;
he'll mount the cross and die to show
    the extremity of God's love!

Jesus, you give me your body to eat,
    even your blood to drink!
In your Eucharist you truly are
    the Son-of-Man-in-me!

Peter's Valiant Boast

Mt 26:31-35: *Then Jesus said to them, "You will all be-*
come deserters because of me this night; for it is written,
 'I will strike the shepherd,
  and the sheep of the flock will be scattered.'
But after I am raised up, I will go ahead of you to Gali-
lee." Peter said to him, "Though all become deserters be-
cause of you, I will never desert you." Jesus said to him,
"Truly I tell you, this very night, before the cock crows,
you will deny me three times." Peter said to him, "Even
though I must die with you, I will not deny you." And
so said all the disciples.

To contemplate:

You interpret Zechariah (13:7),
   telling what will happen now:
God will let you, his people's shepherd,
   be mysteriously struck down,
   and his chosen sheep be scattered!

Before the events occur, you know
   the whole scenario.
Yet ever forward you press on,
   to fulfill God's holy will.

But Peter, ignorant, blundering rock,
   knows better than his Lord:
"Though all the others leave you, Lord,
   I never will desert you!"
Though you warn him with the detail
   of his threefold denial
this very night before cock-crow—
   his rash promise he repeats,
repeats it with such emphasis
   it becomes a flagrant boast:
"Even though I must die with you,
   I will not deny you!"
And so they all follow Peter,
   leader in their boast—
so little do they know themselves,
   that they misplace their trust.

Peter still must learn the truth:
   his utter helplessness
without you to guide him on his way—
   his utter need of you
   to shepherd his every step!

Your Will Be Done

Mt 26:36-46: *Then Jesus went with them to a place called Gethsemane; and he said to his disciples, "Sit here while I go over there and pray." He took with him Peter and the two sons of Zebedee, and began to be grieved and agitated. Then he said to them, "I am deeply grieved, even to death; remain here, and stay awake with me." And going a little farther, he threw himself on the ground and prayed, "My Father, if it is possible, let this cup pass from me; yet not what I want but what you want." Then he came to the disciples and found them sleeping; and he said to Peter, "So, could you not stay awake with me one hour? Stay awake and pray that you may not come into the time of trial; the spirit indeed is willing, but the flesh is weak." Again he went away for the second time and prayed, "My Father, if this cannot pass unless I drink it, your will be done." Again he came and found them sleeping, for their eyes were heavy. So leaving them again, he went away and prayed for the third time, saying the same words. Then he came to the disciples and said to them, "Are you still sleeping and taking your rest? See, the hour is at hand, and the Son of Man is betrayed into the hands of sinners. Get up, let us be going. See, my betrayer is at hand."*

To contemplate:

How penetrating, this glimpse
   into the sorrowing heart of Christ.
      He grieves in death-gripped agony,
   sadly begs his most trusted men
to stay awake and pray with him.
At least he can count on Peter
   to stick by him in his grief.
      "Ah, Peter of sleep-heavy eyes,
   not even an hour's watch with me?
Willing spirit but weakening flesh!"

Long, long ago Isaiah promised
   God would hear his people's plea
      and calm those drunk with anguish:
   "I take from trembling hand the cup,
the cup of staggering—drink no more" (Is 51:21-22).

So Jesus pleads now with his Father
   to let this bitter cup pass by,
      a cup he sees more clearly now—
   last cup of sorrow in his path.
His Father does not take this cup away!

One thing holds his firm resolve,
   one only thing—his Father's will.
      "Your will be done" he cries,
      "Your holy will be done!"

"My Father Could Send Me Legions of Angels"

Mt 26:47-54: *While he was still speaking, Judas, one of the twelve, arrived; with him was a large crowd with swords and clubs, from the chief priests and the elders of the people. Now the betrayer had given them a sign, saying, "The one I will kiss is the man; arrest him." At once he came up to Jesus and said, "Greetings, Rabbi!" and kissed him. Jesus said to him, "Friend, do what you are here to do." Then they came and laid hands on Jesus and arrested him. Suddenly, one of those with Jesus put his hand on his sword, drew it, and struck the slave of the high priest, cutting off his ear. Then Jesus said to him, "Put your sword back into its place; for all who take the sword will perish by the sword. Do you think that I cannot appeal to my Father, and he will at once send me more than twelve legions of angels? But how then would the scriptures be fulfilled, which say it must happen in this way?"*

To contemplate:

In this decisive moment of his life
   his twelve are there with him,
     eleven backing him—

one attacking him
      with kiss.
In his sermon he had told them all,
   "Do not resist the evil one"
   and "Love your enemy":
      he calls his traitor
         "friend."
Then someone swings a mighty sword,
   cuts off protruding ear.
   Stand back, you knaves,
      from warrior bold—
         our Peter!
"Put back your sword! Who takes the sword
   will perish by the same.
   In place of you twelve men
      my Father could send
      angel legions twelve."

O Jesus, how could you give yourself
   to evil men without a fight?
   Why not at least flee from them
      into the night?

"The scriptures must be fulfilled—they say
   it all must happen just this way.
   My Father, your will
      be done!"

Jesus Was Silent

Mt 26:55-63: *At that hour Jesus said to the crowds, "Have you come out with swords and clubs to arrest me as though I were a bandit? Day after day I sat in the temple teaching, and you did not arrest me. But all this has taken place, so that the scriptures of the prophets may be fulfilled." Then all the disciples deserted him and fled.*

Those who had arrested Jesus took him to Caiaphas the high priest, in whose house the scribes and the elders had gathered.... Now the chief priests and the whole council were looking for false testimony against Jesus so that they might put him to death, but they found none, though many false witnesses came forward. At last two came forward and said, "This fellow said, 'I am able to destroy the temple of God and to build it in three days.'" The high priest stood up and said, "Have you no answer? What is it that they testify against you?" But Jesus was silent.

To contemplate:

"This has taken place, the scripture to fulfill."
  Jesus, are you telling us

that you're living out the plan of God,
 formed from long ago?
"Then all the disciples deserted him and fled."
 Earlier this same dark night
Peter had declared, "Though all desert,
 I swear I never will!"
We promise bold actions we often can't fulfill.
 God promised the unbelievable,
  and now you're carrying out his promise
   to the smallest letter.
God's plan advances act by act into its final scenes.
  Chief priests call their witnesses;
 falsely they accuse you of grievous plot
  to destroy God's temple.

They charge that you, true temple, plot to wreck
 yourself.
  Lord, how right they almost are—
 you'll give your body to executioners
  and die upon a cross.
For so has God decreed the climax of his scroll.
 Jesus, you stand before them all,
  silent.
 "Like a sheep before the shearers,
  silent."
 But in your heart you shout:
 "Father, your will be done."

He Deserves Death!

Mt 26:63-68: *Then the high priest said to him, "I put you under oath before the living God, tell us if you are the Messiah, the Son of God." Jesus said to him, "You have said so. But I tell you,*

From now on you will see the Son of Man
seated at the right hand of Power
and coming on the clouds of heaven."

Then the high priest tore his clothes and said, "He has blasphemed! Why do we still need witnesses? You have now heard his blasphemy. What is your verdict?" They answered, "He deserves death." Then they spat in his face and struck him; and some slapped him, saying, "Prophesy to us, you Messiah! Who...struck you?"

To contemplate:

False witnesses accuse you, Lord,
    of plot to destroy their temple;
you maintain your silent calm,
    refuse to defend yourself.
The high priest charges you with oath
    to tell them who you are;

you answer with the Scripture text
    about the Son of Man.
How can they fail to understand,
    if they know the text so well?
You tell your judges about their judge—
    yourself, the Son of God!

"Blasphemy!" they all shout back;
    "What is the verdict now?"
And then they give their harsh decree:
    "Death—we give him death!"
Thus do we kill the awesome truth
    we know we can't control,
reverse creation with destruction,
    preferring death to life.
They spit in your face and strike your cheek,
    strike the face of God-with-us!
Yet you do not strike them back,
    but silently endure their blows.

And do I spit into your face, my Lord?
    Do I strike you on the cheek?
I humbly bow before your face!

    O, be my saving Lord!

Reactions to Jesus of Nazareth

Mt 26:69-27:7: *Now Peter was sitting outside in the courtyard. A servant-girl came to him and said, "You also were with Jesus the Galilean." But he denied it before all of them.... Another servant-girl saw him, and she said to the bystanders, "This man was with Jesus of Nazareth." Again he denied it with an oath.... After a little while the bystanders came up and said to Peter, "Certainly you are also one of them, for your accent betrays you." Then he began to curse, and he swore an oath, "I do not know the man!" At that moment the cock crowed. Then Peter remembered what Jesus had said: "Before the cock crows, you will deny me three times." And he went out and wept bitterly....*

When Judas, his betrayer, saw that Jesus was condemned, he repented and brought back the thirty pieces of silver to the chief priests and the elders. He said, "I have sinned by betraying innocent blood." But they said, "What is that to us? See to it yourself." Throwing down the pieces of silver in the temple, he departed; and he went and hanged himself.

But the chief priests, taking the pieces of silver, said, "It is not lawful to put them into the treasury, since they are blood money." After conferring together, they used them to buy the potter's field as a place to bury foreigners....

To contemplate:

Three times the valiant Peter
　　denies he knows his Lord.
　　　　How true! He knows him not
　　　　　　as man of sacrifice.
By contrast, Judas said
　　he could point out his Lord.
　　　　How true! He led the mob,
　　　　　　as signal kissed his Lord.
Both men are sorry for their act.
　　Peter goes out and weeps for it.
　　　　Judas returns his thirty coins,
　　　　　　then goes and hangs himself.
And what of the temple priests
　　who take the money from the bribe,
　　　　unlawful for temple treasury,
　　　　　　and give it all to charity?

And where am I among these three?
　　Is my charity sincere—from the heart?
　　　　Is my hope an anchor for a deeper trust in God?
　　　　　　Better than denying Peter?

　　Is my faith a light that leads
　　others to the Lord?

Mt 27:11-18 = Mk 15:2-10 Pilate questions Jesus and offers to release Jesus or Barabbas.

That Innocent Man!— Let Him Be Crucified!

Mt 27:19-23: *While he [Pilate] was sitting on the judgment seat, his wife sent word to him, "Have nothing to do with that innocent man, for today I have suffered a great deal because of a dream about him." Now the chief priests and the elders persuaded the crowds to ask for Barabbas and to have Jesus killed. The governor again said to them, "Which of the two do you want me to release for you?" And they said, "Barabbas." Pilate said to them, "Then what should I do with Jesus who is called the Messiah?" All of them said, "Let him be crucified!" Then he asked, "Why, what evil has he done?" But they shouted all the more, "Let him be crucified!"*

To contemplate:

Again a contrast of reactions:
   to Pilate's wife
     Jesus is "innocent";
   but to the crowd
     he's culpable,
so guilty they demand his death:
     "Crucify him!"

Poor Pilate, torn between the two,
offers compromise:
Jesus or Barabbas—
Bar Abba means
Son of the father—
"Choose between two of the Father's sons:
the true one or the false."

The crowd, persuaded by the leaders,
choose Barabbas,
the false son,
over Jesus, the true.
So Pilate asks
"What should I do with Jesus, your Messiah?"
"Crucify him!"

And which do I choose, Jesus or Barabbas,
the true one or the false?
Do I stand for Emmanuel
or Barabbas—
for Savior or murderer?

Lord Jesus, I choose you,
true Son-of-God-with-me!

Pilate Washes His Hands

Mt 27:24-26: *So when Pilate saw that he could do nothing, but rather that a riot was beginning, he took some water and washed his hands before the crowd, saying, "I am innocent of this man's blood; see to it yourselves." Then the people as a whole answered, "His blood be on us and on our children!" So he released Barabbas for them; and after flogging Jesus, he handed him over to be crucified.*

To contemplate:

Pilate washes his hands
    of the whole bloody mess.
Then he hands over the gentle Jesus
    to be flogged and crucified.
The people, whom Jesus shepherded
    and taught and healed and fed,
now make up the crowd that wants his blood,
    lifeblood poured out in death.

Like Pilate, do I feign neutrality,
    stand indifferently aside
and let others violate the truth?
Or like the people, do I let myself
    be led from way of truth?
O Jesus, let me neither be
    Pilate, the "neutral" witness,
nor one who simply follows the crowd.

O Jesus, you shed your blood for me;
may your precious blood save me!

They Mocked Him

Mt 27:27-31: *Then the soldiers of the governor took Jesus into the governor's headquarters, and they gathered the whole cohort around him. They stripped him and put a scarlet robe on him, and after twisting some thorns into a crown, they put it on his head. They put a reed in his right hand and knelt before him and mocked him, saying, "Hail, King of the Jews!" They spat on him, and took the reed and struck him on the head. After mocking him, they stripped him of the robe and put his own clothes on him. Then they led him away to crucify him.*

To contemplate:

What king was ever treated thus
   by those who were his troops?
Only the very King of kings,
   the Savior of the world!

"Off with his clothes, his dignity;
   give him cloak of shame.
Beat him down to our lowly plane;
   we can't abide his rule.

Our king he thinks himself to be?
    Clothe him like one of us,
and make for him a royal crown
    of radiating thorns.
Put in his hand his ruling rod
    and kneel before his face
to offer courtly adulation
    and hail him as our king.
Then spit upon his kingly face
    and strike him with his rod;
strike him on his bleeding head,
    drive deep the piercing thorns."

Some stand aside and laugh at him;
    some indulge brutality.
And when they've had their fill of fun,
    they lead him off to Calvary.

O Jesus, my dear suffering Lord,
    I humbly bow before my king;
you, by enduring this soldiers' farce,
    prove yourself the King of kings.
I picture you in front of me,
    head crowned with piercing thorns,
your scepter in you ruling hand,
    my king, my God-with-me!

They Crucified Him

Mt 27:32-37: *As they went out, they came upon a man from Cyrene named Simon; they compelled this man to carry his cross. And when they came to a place called Golgotha (which means Place of a Skull), they offered him wine to drink, mixed with gall; but when he tasted it, he would not drink it. And when they had crucified him, they divided his clothes among themselves by casting lots; then they sat down there and kept watch over him. Over his head they put the charge against him, which read, "This is Jesus, the King of the Jews."*

To contemplate:

Too weak to bear his cross aloft,
   Jesus needs Simon's help—
but Peter is nowhere to be found;
   they draft another Simon.
Jesus, you told us all so clear:
   "Whoever would follow me
must take up his cross and carry it
   faithfully after me."

Now no disciple bears your cross;
    in your hour of greatest need.
The soldiers force a passerby
    to help you on your way.

At Golgotha they offer you
    wine mixed with bitter gall,
but you refuse the deadening drink,
    to taste the Father's cup.
And then they crucify you, Lord,
    fix you to your cross,
to hang for all to see and mock,
    no more to walk the earth.
They fix you to the cross, my Lord,
    with cruelly piercing nails.
They gamble for your clothes, my king.
    Who will flaunt your royal cloak?
"This is Jesus, King of Jews,"
    so reads the sign that tells
what's really happening here,
    my Jesus, King of kings!

I look upon my crucifix,
    yet seldom do I *see*—
seldom see my Lord hang there—
    his blood, his sweat, his tears.
My crucified, live within my heart!

He Cannot Save Himself

Mt 27:38-44: *Then two bandits were crucified with him, one on his right and one on his left. Those who passed by derided him, shaking their heads and saying, "You who would destroy the temple and build it in three days, save yourself! If you are the Son of God, come down from the cross." In the same way the chief priests also, along with the scribes and elders, were mocking him, saying, "He saved others; he cannot save himself. He is the King of Israel; let him come down from the cross now, and we will believe in him. He trusts in God; let God deliver him now, if he wants to; for he said, 'I am God's Son.'" The bandits who were crucified with him also taunted him in the same way.*

To contemplate:

You hang upon your cross,
   two bandits at your side;
the three of you in life
   and death—criminals.
You hang there helplessly,
   unable to take a step

or even loose one hand
   to save a dying man.
"If you are the Son of God,
   come down from the cross,"
thus passers-by deride you,
   shaking their wiser heads.
"He saved so many others,
   yet cannot save himself";
thus those who stand and mock
   exult in their ridicule.
And even the poor lost bandits,
   dying there with you,
taunt you to save yourself,
   and with you, save them too.
None there to comfort you;
   no one believes in you.
Only enemies surround you
   with taunts and mockery:
"O helpless Lord upon a cross,
   between heaven and earth;
we have you where we want you,
   commandment-giving God!"

Yet even as they triumph
   in fight with you, their Lord,
your helplessness reveals you—
   truly one like us!

My God, My God!

Mt 27:45-50: *From noon on, darkness came over the whole land until three in the afternoon. And about three o'clock Jesus cried with a loud voice, "Eli, Eli, lema sabachthani?" that is, "My God, my God, why have you forsaken me?" When some of the bystanders heard it, they said, "This man is calling for Elijah." At once one of them ran and got a sponge, filled it with sour wine, put it on a stick, and gave it to him to drink. But the others said, "Wait, let us see whether Elijah will come to save him." Then Jesus cried again with a loud voice and breathed his last.*

To contemplate:

Darkness, the darkness of the evil one,
   covers the whole wide world.
     Is it the black hour
of victory of evil over good—
the hour of Satan's triumph over God?
For now the evil one has God's only Son
   transfixed upon the cross
     in final agony.

But the throne of God is silent still.
  Only the Son of God cries out,
    "My God, my God,
  why have you forsaken me?"
No answer from the throne above.

The silence of God is shattering.
  Is there a God up there at all?
    Or is it just a lie
  worse than Satan's lies?
Is there no God to answer—just a void?
If God's not there, where did Elijah go?
  And if God can't help his Son,
    how can Elijah help?
  Jesus hangs there helplessly,
listening vainly for answer to his call.
This is the test, the final test of all.
  The answer to his dying prayer
    is soul-emptying silence!
  Yet Jesus cries aloud once more,
and dies, dies with loud cry to his Father.

What is his last cry of death?
  "Father, your will be done!"
    Thus dies the Son of God.

Truly This Man Was God's Son!

Mt 27:50-56: *Then Jesus cried again with a loud voice and breathed his last. At that moment the curtain of the temple was torn in two, from top to bottom. The earth shook, and the rocks were split. The tombs also were opened, and many bodies of the saints who had fallen asleep were raised. After his resurrection they came out of the tombs and entered the holy city and appeared to many. Now when the centurion and those with him, who were keeping watch over Jesus, saw the earthquake and what took place, they were terrified and said, "Truly this man was God's Son!"*

Many women were also there, looking on from a distance; they had followed Jesus from Galilee and had provided for him. Among them were Mary Magdalene, and Mary the mother of James and Joseph, and the mother of the sons of Zebedee.

To contemplate:

Powerful portents greet the death of Jesus:

The curtain hiding holy place is torn apart,
    unveiling God for humankind to find—
        Jesus' death bares God's love!

The death of Jesus shatters more than earth—
it shakes even our stagnant souls,
splits our rock-hard hearts.

It splits open tombs of his chosen dead,
raises bodies from their graves
anticipating resurrection.
Even Roman soldiers read these signs:
they cry aloud the meaning clear:
"This man was God's Son!"
More valiant than his manly followers,
women who followed him from Galilee
watch all these happenings.

O Jesus, hanging dead upon the cross,
I would be there with you,
absorbed in deepest prayer.
The mystery of your death defies our grasp.
How could our saving God-with-us
just—die?

If you, our source of health and life,
could die such a horrible death,
then I can face death too—
but only if I truly die in you,
only if then you'll be my saving God-with-me.

Mt 27:57-61 = Mk 15:42-47 The burial of Jesus.

They Sealed the Tomb

Mt 27:62-66: *The next day [after Joseph of Arimathea had laid the body of Jesus in his new tomb], that is, after the day of Preparation, the chief priests and the Pharisees gathered before Pilate and said, "Sir, we remember what that impostor said while he was still alive, 'After three days I will rise again.' Therefore command the tomb to be made secure until the third day; otherwise his disciples may go and steal him away, and tell the people, 'He has been raised from the dead,' and the last deception would be worse than the first." Pilate said to them, "You have a guard of soldiers; go, make it as secure as you can." So they went with the guard and made the tomb secure by sealing the stone.*

To contemplate:

Not enough to hang him on the cross
    and watch until he breathed his last.
Not enough to lay him in a tomb
    and close it with a giant stone.
They must seal the stone and place a guard,
    lest his disciples steal his body

and claim he's risen from the dead,
    risen, as they recall he said.
Strange irony: his enemies remember
    what his disciples now forget.
His enemies do more to seal him up,
    than his disciples to bring him out.

Has it not been ever thus, my Lord?
    Your enemies' zeal to shut you up,
is greater than your followers' fire
    to spread your saving word abroad.
While your disciples hide in fear,
    your adversaries take the field
and bravely stand their ground around
    a dead man's tomb, to keep him there.
As though you need the help of fraud
    to win your cause with humankind!
You could always send your angel legions
    to take the place of your poor men.

Yet your body lies within its tomb,
    unmoving, silent, still in death,
the body of my saving Lord—
    holy body clothed in death.
    O saving God-with-me,
    I fall silent, too.

He Has Been Raised!

Mt 28:1-7: *After the sabbath, as the first day of the week was dawning, Mary Magdalene and the other Mary went to see the tomb. And suddenly there was a great earthquake; for an angel of the Lord, descending from heaven, came and rolled back the stone and sat on it. His appearance was like lightning, and his clothing white as snow. For fear of him the guards shook and became like dead men. But the angel said to the women, "Do not be afraid; I know that you are looking for Jesus who was crucified. He is not here; for he has been raised, as he said. Come, see the place where he lay. Then go quickly and tell his disciples, 'He has been raised from the dead, and indeed he is going ahead of you to Galilee; there you will see him.' This is my message for you."*

To contemplate:

Another quake of earth announces
   another great event.
     One heavenly angel,
   enough to shake the earth
and all the soldiers with it.

The guards become like men in death,
    as Jesus rises up to life.
        They see him not,
    but only lightning bolt
of angel clothed in white.
The angel ignores the shaking men
    and, turning to the women,
        announces Jesus
    has risen from the dead,
risen as he three times said.
"Come and see the empty tomb,
    and tell his followers
        he's gone to Galilee;
    he'll see them there again
in the place where it all began."

Oh, Easter joy! Oh, angel voice,
    that tells the great event,
        the core event
    of the history of the world—
the resurrection of its Lord!
Transfiguration of life itself—
    this change makes others
        insignificant.
    Jesus is alive again
but with new life transcending old.
    My risen God-in-me!

Tell My Brothers

Mt 28:8-10: *So they [the women] left the tomb quickly with fear and great joy, and ran to tell his disciples. Suddenly Jesus met them and said, "Greetings!" And they came to him, took hold of his feet, and worshiped him. Then Jesus said to them, "Do not be afraid; go and tell my brothers to go to Galilee; there they will see me."*

To contemplate:

Imagine being greeted by the Lord!
   "Greetings," he says
     to the women,
  the first he favors
with his glorious, risen presence.
   They come to him,
   take hold of him,
     and worship him.
They have never worshiped him before;
   but now their first impulse
     on seeing him risen
   is to adore and worship him—
they recognize their Lord-with-them.

"Don't be afraid;
tell my brothers
   to go to Galilee
   to see me there."
Now he calls his disciples *"brothers."*

O Brother Jesus, to the world's end
   I'd go to hold you
and never let you go from me,
if only I could live with you, my Lord.
   "Don't be afraid
   of losing me;
   I live with you,
      I live in you—
      I am Emmanuel!"

Jesus, I recall your solemn promise:
   "What you do for your brother or sister,
      you do for me."
   I do not have to go anywhere
to find you, hold you, worship you:
   you live with me;
   you live in me—
      you are my saving
      God-within!

Tale of the Guards

Mt 28:11-15: *While they [the women Jesus sent] were going, some of the guard went into the city and told the chief priests everything that had happened. After the priests had assembled with the elders, they devised a plan to give a large sum of money to the soldiers, telling them, "You must say, 'His disciples came by night and stole him away while we were asleep.' If this comes to the governor's ears, we will satisfy him and keep you out of trouble." So they took the money and did as they were directed.*

To contemplate:

When the soldiers give their report
   of what happened at the tomb
they are told to hush up the truth
   with a story that is false.

It matters not their story makes no sense—
   that men can't see reality in sleep—
reality no longer interests them;
   they cover up what they know is true.

Is it not ever thus, dear Lord?
  Do we not make up our own "truth," too?

Our great temptation, Lord of truth—
  to put our faith in the ultimate untruth,
that earthly life completes
  reality; we need no more!

And so, we grow quite capable
  of disregarding the further life
you offer through your resurrection:
  life in you, your Father, and the Spirit.

Dear Lord of life beyond the grave,
  increase my resurrection faith.

Let me hold to the greatest truth:
  that you have risen from the dead.

And grant that I may rise with you
  to your new life beyond the grave,

beginning now to live with you,
  my risen Lord who lives in me!

They Worshiped Him

Mt 28:16-18: *Now the eleven disciples went to Galilee, to the mountain to which Jesus had directed them. When they saw him, they worshiped him; but some doubted. And Jesus came and said to them, "All authority in heaven and on earth has been given to me."*

To contemplate:

They return to Galilee—
   transfiguration mount—
      where he had first revealed
      the beauty that is his.
For precious fleeting moments
   they would faintly glimpse
      the glory he could claim—
      glory of divinity!
To live our human state,
   Jesus had emptied himself
      of his divine control,
         to embrace our slavery (Phil 2:7).

But now his glory shines
　　through his human state;
　　　　down they fall prostrate
　　　　　　and worship him as God.
Yet even in this moment
　　of delirious delight,
　　　　they waver in their doubt.
　　　　　　"Oh, is it really true?"
He lovingly assures them,
　　"Yes, it's true, all power
　　　　in heaven and earth is mine,
　　　　　　all authority to rule."

O Jesus, I believe in you,
　　and with your first disciples
　　　　fall down to worship you,
　　　　　　acknowledging your glory.
I believe in all your words;
　　I love your every act;
　　　　I embrace your very life
　　　　　　and hope to be with you.

The foundation of my faith
　　and hope and love and life
　　　　is your resurrection, Lord,
　　　　　　O glorious God-with-me!

I Am with You Always

Mt 28:19-20: *"Go therefore and make disciples of all nations, baptizing them in the name of the Father and of the Son and of the Holy Spirit, and teaching them to obey everything that I have commanded you. And remember, I am with you always, to the end of the age."*

To contemplate:

Jesus commissions his disciples
   to become apostles now
to all the nations of the earth,
   baptizing and teaching them.
A new age is here proclaimed
   by the Maker of all the ages,
an age to last to the end of time,
   age of his Church's mission.
It is the age of the Trinity—
   the Father, Son, and Spirit—
in whom disciples of all nations
   are called to be baptized.
But Lord, how can eleven men
   go out to all the world—

men who could not stand with you
    on the hill of Calvary?
How can eleven men defeat
    the tempter of humankind,
and bring all men and women truth
    that they themselves can doubt?
Only if, with their little faith,
    they still believe in you
who promise to remain with them
    until the end of time.

And we who have received their word
    and carried it in ourselves,
how can we, weak as we are,
    be wholly true to you?
O Jesus, our saving Emmanuel,
    brace up our wavering faith;
O Jesus, truly our God-with-us,
    sustain our fragile hope.

O Jesus, our glorious risen Lord,
    fill us with your love,
a love so strong and so steadfast,
    it will shine even through us.

Jesus Is God-with-Us to the End!

Ah, Matthew, thank you for your strong portrait
   of Jesus in his acts and words—his life.

You reveal him as our truly human brother,
   complete member of Abraham's family tree—
a man like us, subjected to temptation
   and vulnerable as we to violent death.

But from the start you tell us he is more,
   much more than any other human being.
His name, "Jesus," means Savior of our race,
   for he's Emmanuel, our saving God-with-us!

Though master of unequaled divine wisdom,
   he treats disciples as his equal brothers;
though suffering hunger and fatigue with them,
   he possesses godly inner power.

He comes to them walking on churning waves,
   heartens Peter to try to do the same;
and when impetuous Peter falters in attempt,
   holds him up, saves him from the deep.

He tells them he is with them to the end:
   "So whoever welcomes you, welcomes me;

who comes to you with heavy heart, comes to me—
　　with your embrace, I also lift him up!"

O Jesus, our hearts are often weighted down
　　with the foolish worries of our broken world;
lift us above the swirling waves of anguish
　　and hold us close, as you held Peter.

"Where two or three are gathered in my name,
　　there am I among you," so you said.
And we believe and gather in your name,
　　secure in your presence here within us now.

For you, who are so meek and gentle-hearted,
　　promised refreshment to our thirsting souls;
you do not break the bruised reed of our hearts,
　　nor quench the wick of our faintly flickering
　　　　hopes.

When we come to you to rest our weary souls,
　　we know that you are really there for us,
no, *here* with us, within our heavy hearts;
　　before we come to you, you've come to us!

And when we want to touch your sacred heart,
　　we reach out just to touch another's heart,
full of confidence in your sacred word:
　　"As you do to another, you also do to me!"

From first to last you are our human brother,
　　from first to last you are our divine Lord—

the God of Israel, the God of the human race,
   the God who made and loves and cares for us.

Yet you're not the God who lives so far away
   that we can never hope to reach your heart;
though you ascended to your Father's throne
   and there now dwell in everlasting light—
   you are Emmanuel, our saving God-with-us!

BOOKS & MEDIA

The Daughters of St. Paul operate book and media centers at the following addresses. Visit, call or write the one nearest you today, or find us on the World Wide Web, www.pauline.org

CALIFORNIA
3908 Sepulveda Blvd., Culver City, CA 90230; 310-397-8676
5945 Balboa Ave., San Diego, CA 92111; 619-565-9181
46 Geary Street, San Francisco, CA 94108; 415-781-5180

FLORIDA
145 S.W. 107th Ave., Miami, FL 33174; 305-559-6715

HAWAII
1143 Bishop Street, Honolulu, HI 96813; 808-521-2731

ILLINOIS
172 North Michigan Ave., Chicago, IL 60601; 312-346-4228

LOUISIANA
4403 Veterans Memorial Blvd., Metairie, LA 70006; 504-887-7631

MASSACHUSETTS
Rte. 1, 885 Providence Hwy., Dedham, MA 02026; 781-326-5385

MISSOURI
9804 Watson Rd., St. Louis, MO 63126; 314-965-3512

NEW JERSEY
561 U.S. Route 1, Wick Plaza, Edison, NJ 08817; 732-572-1200

NEW YORK
150 East 52nd Street, New York, NY 10022; 212-754-1110
78 Fort Place, Staten Island, NY 10301; 718-447-5071

OHIO
2105 Ontario Street (at Prospect Ave.), Cleveland, OH 44115; 440-621-9427

PENNSYLVANIA
9171-A Roosevelt Blvd., Philadelphia, PA 19114; 215-676-9494

SOUTH CAROLINA
243 King Street, Charleston, SC 29401; 843-577-0175

TENNESSEE
4811 Poplar Ave., Memphis, TN 38117 901-761-2987

TEXAS
114 Main Plaza, San Antonio, TX 78205; 210-224-8101

VIRGINIA
1025 King Street, Alexandria, VA 22314; 703-549-3806

CANADA
3022 Dufferin Street, Toronto, Ontario, Canada M6B 3T5; 416-781-9131
1155 Yonge Street, Toronto, Ontario, Canada M4T 1W2; 416-934-3440

¡Libros en español!